Pentecostalism: A Very Short Introduction

VERY SHORT INTRODUCTIONS are for anyone wanting a stimulating and accessible way into a new subject. They are written by experts, and have been translated into more than 45 different languages.

The series began in 1995, and now covers a wide variety of topics in every discipline. The VSI library now contains over 500 volumes—a Very Short Introduction to everything from Psychology and Philosophy of Science to American History and Relativity—and continues to grow in every subject area.

Titles in the series include the following:

AFRICAN HISTORY John Parker and
    Richard Rathbone
AGEING Nancy A. Pachana
ALGEBRA Peter M. Higgins
AMERICAN HISTORY Paul S. Boyer
AMERICAN IMMIGRATION
    David A. Gerber
AMERICAN LEGAL HISTORY
    G. Edward White
AMERICAN POLITICAL HISTORY
    Donald Critchlow
AMERICAN POLITICAL PARTIES
    AND ELECTIONS L. Sandy Maisel
AMERICAN POLITICS
    Richard M. Valelly
THE AMERICAN PRESIDENCY
    Charles O. Jones
AMERICAN SLAVERY
    Heather Andrea Williams
ANARCHISM Colin Ward
ANCIENT EGYPT Ian Shaw
ANCIENT GREECE Paul Cartledge
THE ANCIENT NEAR EAST
    Amanda H. Podany
ANCIENT PHILOSOPHY Julia Annas
ANCIENT WARFARE Harry Sidebottom
ANGLICANISM Mark Chapman
THE ANGLO-SAXON AGE John Blair
ANIMAL BEHAVIOUR
    Tristram D. Wyatt
ANIMAL RIGHTS David DeGrazia
ANXIETY Daniel Freeman and
    Jason Freeman
ARCHAEOLOGY Paul Bahn

ARISTOTLE Jonathan Barnes
ART HISTORY Dana Arnold
ART THEORY Cynthia Freeland
ASTROPHYSICS James Binney
ATHEISM Julian Baggini
THE ATMOSPHERE Paul I. Palmer
AUGUSTINE Henry Chadwick
BACTERIA Sebastian G. B. Amyes
BARTHES Jonathan Culler
BEAUTY Roger Scruton
THE BIBLE John Riches
BLACK HOLES Katherine Blundell
BLOOD Chris Cooper
THE BRAIN Michael O'Shea
THE BRICS Andrew F. Cooper
BRITISH POLITICS Anthony Wright
BUDDHA Michael Carrithers
BUDDHISM Damien Keown
BUDDHIST ETHICS Damien Keown
BYZANTIUM Peter Sarris
CANCER Nicholas James
CAPITALISM James Fulcher
CATHOLICISM Gerald O'Collins
THE CELTS Barry Cunliffe
CHEMISTRY Peter Atkins
CHOICE THEORY Michael Allingham
CHRISTIANITY Linda Woodhead
CIRCADIAN RHYTHMS Russell Foster
    and Leon Kreitzman
CITIZENSHIP Richard Bellamy
CLASSICAL MYTHOLOGY
    Helen Morales
CLASSICS Mary Beard and
    John Henderson

CLIMATE Mark Maslin
CLIMATE CHANGE Mark Maslin
THE COLD WAR Robert McMahon
COMBINATORICS Robin Wilson
COMMUNISM Leslie Holmes
COMPUTER SCIENCE Subrata Dasgupta
CONSCIOUSNESS Susan Blackmore
CONTEMPORARY ART
    Julian Stallabrass
CORAL REEFS Charles Sheppard
COSMOLOGY Peter Coles
THE CRUSADES Christopher Tyerman
DADA AND SURREALISM
    David Hopkins
DANTE Peter Hainsworth and
    David Robey
DARWIN Jonathan Howard
THE DEAD SEA SCROLLS
    Timothy Lim
DECOLONIZATION Dane Kennedy
DEMOCRACY Bernard Crick
DESIGN John Heskett
DINOSAURS David Norman
DREAMING J. Allan Hobson
DRUGS Les Iversen
DRUIDS Barry Cunliffe
THE EARTH Martin Redfern
ECONOMICS Partha Dasgupta
EGYPTIAN MYTH Geraldine Pinch
THE ELEMENTS Philip Ball
EMOTION Dylan Evans
EMPIRE Stephen Howe
ENGLISH LITERATURE Jonathan Bate
THE ENLIGHTENMENT
    John Robertson
EPICUREANISM Catherine Wilson
EPIDEMIOLOGY Rodolfo Saracci
ETHICS Simon Blackburn
EUGENICS Philippa Levine
THE EUROPEAN UNION John Pinder
    and Simon Usherwood
EVOLUTION Brian and
    Deborah Charlesworth
EXISTENTIALISM Thomas Flynn
FASCISM Kevin Passmore
FEMINISM Margaret Walters
THE FIRST WORLD WAR
    Michael Howard
FORENSIC PSYCHOLOGY
    David Canter

FOUCAULT Gary Gutting
FREE SPEECH Nigel Warburton
FREE WILL Thomas Pink
FREUD Anthony Storr
FUNDAMENTALISM Malise Ruthven
FUNGI Nicholas P. Money
GALAXIES John Gribbin
GALILEO Stillman Drake
GAME THEORY Ken Binmore
GANDHI Bhikhu Parekh
GEOGRAPHY John Matthews and
    David Herbert
GEOPOLITICS Klaus Dodds
GLOBAL CATASTROPHES Bill McGuire
GLOBAL ECONOMIC HISTORY
    Robert C. Allen
GLOBALIZATION Manfred Steger
GOD John Bowker
HABERMAS James Gordon Finlayson
HEGEL Peter Singer
HINDUISM Kim Knott
HISTORY John H. Arnold
THE HISTORY OF LIFE Michael Benton
THE HISTORY OF MATHEMATICS
    Jacqueline Stedall
THE HISTORY OF MEDICINE
    William Bynum
THE HISTORY OF TIME
    Leofranc Holford-Strevens
HIV AND AIDS Alan Whiteside
HOLLYWOOD Peter Decherney
HUMAN ANATOMY
    Leslie Klenerman
HUMAN EVOLUTION Bernard Wood
HUMAN RIGHTS Andrew Clapham
IDEOLOGY Michael Freeden
INDIAN PHILOSOPHY Sue Hamilton
INFINITY Ian Stewart
INFORMATION Luciano Floridi
INNOVATION Mark Dodgson and
    David Gann
INTELLIGENCE Ian J. Deary
INTERNATIONAL
    MIGRATION Khalid Koser
INTERNATIONAL RELATIONS
    Paul Wilkinson
ISLAM Malise Ruthven
ISLAMIC HISTORY Adam Silverstein
JESUS Richard Bauckham
JOURNALISM Ian Hargreaves

JUDAISM Norman Solomon
JUNG Anthony Stevens
KABBALAH Joseph Dan
KANT Roger Scruton
KNOWLEDGE Jennifer Nagel
THE KORAN Michael Cook
LATE ANTIQUITY Gillian Clark
LAW Raymond Wacks
THE LAWS OF THERMODYNAMICS
    Peter Atkins
LEADERSHIP Keith Grint
LEARNING Mark Haselgrove
LIGHT Ian Walmsley
LINGUISTICS Peter Matthews
LITERARY THEORY Jonathan Culler
LOCKE John Dunn
LOGIC Graham Priest
MACHIAVELLI Quentin Skinner
MARTIN LUTHER Scott H. Hendrix
MARTYRDOM Jolyon Mitchell
MARX Peter Singer
MATHEMATICS Timothy Gowers
THE MEANING OF LIFE Terry Eagleton
MEASUREMENT David Hand
MEDICAL ETHICS Tony Hope
MEDIEVAL BRITAIN John Gillingham
    and Ralph A. Griffiths
MEDIEVAL LITERATURE
    Elaine Treharne
MEDIEVAL PHILOSOPHY
    John Marenbon
MEMORY Jonathan K. Foster
METAPHYSICS Stephen Mumford
MICROSCOPY Terence Allen
MILITARY JUSTICE Eugene R. Fidell
MODERN ART David Cottington
MODERN CHINA Rana Mitter
MODERN IRELAND Senia Pašeta
MODERN ITALY Anna Cento Bull
MODERN JAPAN
    Christopher Goto-Jones
MODERNISM Christopher Butler
MOLECULAR BIOLOGY Aysha Divan
    and Janice A. Royds
MOLECULES Philip Ball
MOONS David A. Rothery
MUSIC Nicholas Cook
MYTH Robert A. Segal
NEOLIBERALISM Manfred Steger and
    Ravi Roy

NEWTON Robert Iliffe
NIETZSCHE Michael Tanner
NORTH AMERICAN INDIANS
    Theda Perdue and Michael D. Green
NORTHERN IRELAND
    Marc Mulholland
NOTHING Frank Close
NUCLEAR PHYSICS Frank Close
NUTRITION David A. Bender
THE PALESTINIAN-ISRAELI
    CONFLICT Martin Bunton
PANDEMICS Christian W. McMillen
PARTICLE PHYSICS Frank Close
THE PERIODIC TABLE Eric R. Scerri
PHILOSOPHY Edward Craig
PHILOSOPHY IN THE ISLAMIC
    WORLD Peter Adamson
PHILOSOPHY OF LAW
    Raymond Wacks
PHILOSOPHY OF SCIENCE
    Samir Okasha
PHOTOGRAPHY Steve Edwards
PHYSICAL CHEMISTRY Peter Atkins
PLANETS David A. Rothery
PLATO Julia Annas
POLITICAL PHILOSOPHY David Miller
POLITICS Kenneth Minogue
POPULISM Cas Mudde and
    Cristóbal Rovira Kaltwasser
POSTCOLONIALISM Robert Young
POSTMODERNISM Christopher Butler
POSTSTRUCTURALISM
    Catherine Belsey
PREHISTORY Chris Gosden
PRESOCRATIC PHILOSOPHY
    Catherine Osborne
PSYCHIATRY Tom Burns
PSYCHOLOGY Gillian Butler and
    Freda McManus
PSYCHOTHERAPY Tom Burns and
    Eva Burns-Lundgren
PUBLIC HEALTH Virginia Berridge
QUANTUM THEORY
    John Polkinghorne
RACISM Ali Rattansi
THE REFORMATION Peter Marshall
RELATIVITY Russell Stannard
THE RENAISSANCE Jerry Brotton
RENAISSANCE ART
    Geraldine A. Johnson

REVOLUTIONS Jack A. Goldstone
RHETORIC Richard Toye
RISK Baruch Fischhoff and John Kadvany
RITUAL Barry Stephenson
RIVERS Nick Middleton
ROBOTICS Alan Winfield
ROMAN BRITAIN Peter Salway
THE ROMAN EMPIRE
    Christopher Kelly
THE ROMAN REPUBLIC
    David M. Gwynn
RUSSIAN HISTORY Geoffrey Hosking
THE RUSSIAN REVOLUTION
    S. A. Smith
SCHIZOPHRENIA Chris Frith and
    Eve Johnstone
SCIENCE AND RELIGION
    Thomas Dixon
SEXUALITY Véronique Mottier
SHAKESPEARE'S COMEDIES
    Bart van Es
SIKHISM Eleanor Nesbitt
SLEEP Steven W. Lockley and
    Russell G. Foster
SOCIAL AND CULTURAL
    ANTHROPOLOGY
    John Monaghan and Peter Just
SOCIAL PSYCHOLOGY Richard J. Crisp
SOCIAL WORK Sally Holland and
    Jonathan Scourfield
SOCIALISM Michael Newman
SOCIOLOGY Steve Bruce

SOCRATES C. C. W. Taylor
SOUND Mike Goldsmith
THE SOVIET UNION Stephen Lovell
THE SPANISH CIVIL WAR
    Helen Graham
SPANISH LITERATURE Jo Labanyi
STATISTICS David J. Hand
STUART BRITAIN John Morrill
SYMMETRY Ian Stewart
TAXATION Stephen Smith
TELESCOPES Geoff Cottrell
TERRORISM Charles Townshend
THEOLOGY David F. Ford
TIBETAN BUDDHISM
    Matthew T. Kapstein
THE TROJAN WAR Eric H. Cline
THE TUDORS John Guy
THE UNITED NATIONS
    Jussi M. Hanhimäki
THE U.S. CONGRESS Donald A. Ritchie
THE U.S. SUPREME COURT
    Linda Greenhouse
THE VIKINGS Julian Richards
VIRUSES Dorothy H. Crawford
WAR AND TECHNOLOGY
    Alex Roland
WILLIAM SHAKESPEARE
    Stanley Wells
WITCHCRAFT Malcolm Gaskill
THE WORLD TRADE
    ORGANIZATION Amrita Narlikar
WORLD WAR II Gerhard L. Weinberg

William K. Kay

PENTECOSTALISM

A Very Short Introduction

OXFORD
UNIVERSITY PRESS

OXFORD
UNIVERSITY PRESS

Great Clarendon Street, Oxford OX2 6DP

Oxford University Press is a department of the University of Oxford.
It furthers the University's objective of excellence in research, scholarship,
and education by publishing worldwide in

Oxford New York

Auckland Cape Town Dar es Salaam Hong Kong Karachi
Kuala Lumpur Madrid Melbourne Mexico City Nairobi
New Delhi Shanghai Taipei Toronto

With offices in

Argentina Austria Brazil Chile Czech Republic France Greece
Guatemala Hungary Italy Japan Poland Portugal Singapore
South Korea Switzerland Thailand Turkey Ukraine Vietnam

Oxford is a registered trade mark of Oxford University Press
in the UK and in certain other countries

Published in the United States
by Oxford University Press Inc., New York

© William K. Kay 2011

The moral rights of the author have been asserted
Database right Oxford University Press (maker)

First published 2011

British Library Cataloguing in Publication Data
Data available

Library of Congress Cataloging in Publication Data
Data available

Typeset by SPI Publisher Services, Pondicherry, India
Printed in Great Britain by
Ashford Colour Press Ltd, Gosport, Hampshire

ISBN: 978-0-19-957515-2

7 9 10 8 6

For Joel

Contents

List of illustrations xiii

Introduction 1

1 Origins and characteristics 3

2 The United States 17

3 Across the world 35

4 Glossolalia, healing, prosperity, and spiritual warfare 57

5 Churches and beliefs about the end of time 74

6 Megachurches, cells, and progressive Pentecostalism 89

7 Race, ecumenism, and politics 106

8 Studies and surveys 120

Further reading 131

Chronology 137

Index 141

List of illustrations

1 Pandita Ramabai **22**
Mary Evans Picture Library

2 The leadership of the Azusa
Street mission **24**
Flower Pentecostal Heritage Center

3 The simple wooden building
on 312 Azusa Street, Los
Angeles **26**
Flower Pentecostal Heritage Center

4 *The Apostolic Faith*
newspaper **29**
Flower Pentecostal Heritage Center

5 Aimee Semple
McPherson **33**
The Granger Collection/TopFoto

6 T. B. Barratt **37**
Flower Pentecostal Heritage Center

7 African Pentecostal-style
churches **49**
Christey Carwile

8 An example of African
Pentecostalism **49**
© Patrick Robert/Sygma/Corbis

9 Minnie Abrams **52**
Flower Pentecostal Heritage Center

10 Francisco Olazábal **54**
Flower Pentecostal Heritage Center

11 Oral Roberts **66**
Flower Pentecostal Heritage Center

12 Smith Wigglesworth **70**
Flower Pentecostal Heritage Center

13 A typical eschatological
chart **76**
© Tim Morton

14 David Yonggi Cho **91**
Flower Pentecostal Heritage Center

15 The Yoido Full Gospel
Church **94**
© Pascal Deloche/Godong/Corbis

16 Hillsongs Church, Australia **100**
Hillsong Church, London

17 Kaka, Brazilian footballer **101**
© Sampics/Corbis

18 Jackie Pullinger **115**
© Art Directors & TRIP/Alamy

19 The 'three waves' of Pentecostalism **122**

Introduction

Pentecostalism is a renewal movement within Christianity. It can be understood as a continuation of a series of renewal movements that go right back to the earliest days of the church. In its modern form, Pentecostalism is usually dated from the start of the 20th century, with immediate roots going back to the 19th century into revivalist Methodism, holiness offshoots of Methodism, Pietism, international missions, and protagonists of divine healing.

What is extraordinary about Pentecostalism in its present existence is that it has encircled the globe. Largely unseen by academic commentators and historians, it managed to survive the wars and tragedies of the 20th century and to cope with all the changes brought about by the clashes between capitalism and communism or between fascism and democracy. During a century when Western Europe became less religious, Pentecostalism and its neo-Pentecostal offshoots radiated across the world following many of the roads taken by Methodism or by later Protestant missionaries. When nations in Africa became independent of their colonial masters after 1945, Christianity remained, often in a Pentecostal form. While Europe was embroiled in mid-century hot and cold wars, Pentecostals were beginning to be established in Latin America and Asia. At the start of the 21st century, Pentecostal churches were to be found all over Latin America in a challenge to the dominance of Roman Catholicism. Even in China, which had largely resisted Christian mission, there were Pentecostal and charismatic churches which emerged blinking from an underground existence once the embargoes of totalitarian communism began to be lifted in the post-Mao era.

The first three chapters that follow are mainly historical; they sketch out the origins and growth of Pentecostalism and show how it spread across the world and its main characteristics. After this, two chapters provide a theological account of Pentecostalism, showing what the main beliefs of Pentecostals are and how they are worked out in local congregations. The next two chapters discuss Pentecostalism from a sociological perspective, outlining its political and humanitarian impulses. The final chapter makes use of recent international statistical surveys to gain an idea of possible future trajectories for Pentecostals and for Christians in general.

The participants in the renewal are found in 740 Pentecostal denominations; 6,530 non-Pentecostal, mainline denominations with large organised internal charismatic movements; and 18,810 independent, neocharismatic denominations and networks. Charismatics are now found across the entire spectrum of Christianity, within all 150 traditional non-Pentecostal ecclesiastical confessions, families, and traditions. Pentecostals/charismatics...are found...speaking in 8,000 languages, and covering [in reach of] 95% of the world's total population.

David Barrett and Todd Johnson, 'Global Statistics', in *The New International Dictionary of Pentecostal and Charismatic Movements*, p. 284

Chapter 1
Origins and characteristics

The first four books of the New Testament are about Jesus Christ and, in these books, about one-third of the content is devoted to his arrest, trial, crucifixion, and resurrection. The fifth book of the New Testament, the Acts of the Apostles, begins with an account of the risen Christ and his promise of the outpouring of the Holy Spirit upon the church. In the second chapter of Acts, the text tells us:

> When the day of Pentecost came, they were all together in one place. Suddenly a sound like the blowing of a violent wind came from heaven and filled the whole house where they were sitting. They saw what seemed to be tongues of fire that separated and came to rest on each of them. All of them were filled with the Holy Spirit and began to speak in other tongues as the Spirit enabled them.

This account of the first Day of Pentecost in the Christian era gives Pentecostalism its name. The account contains a series of themes and motifs that will recur as Pentecostalism unfolds across the 20th century.

The text describes what is clearly a religious experience of the first magnitude. We can analyse this experience into its component parts. The people hear the sound of wind that fills the whole house where they are sitting. This is noteworthy since one would not expect to hear the sound of wind filling the inside of a house but, in any case, the sound of the wind is replaced by the appearance of fire. This fire begins as a single mass of flames that appears somewhere in the room where the 120 people are gathered. Presumably the fire is seen in a collective vision since there is no report of panic or burning. The fire then separates into small flames which rest upon the heads of each person individually. There is therefore a collective experience of fire and an individual experience of fire. The next sentence tells us that they were all filled with the Holy Spirit, and the most natural explanation of the text is that the fire is symbolic of the Holy Spirit. Having rested upon each person, the Spirit now fills each person. We might say that the vision is of the arrival of the Spirit signalled by the sound of wind, the appearance of the Spirit symbolized by fire, and then the experience of the Spirit filling each person. We might also notice the egalitarian nature of the event, in the sense that nobody is singled out above the rest; they are all filled with the Spirit without any distinction between them. What follows next is crucial to an understanding of Pentecostalism.

Once filled with the Holy Spirit, the people 'began to speak in other tongues as the Spirit enabled them'. The text is very specific here. Each individual began to speak in other tongues (or other languages) as the Spirit enabled them. It was not that the Spirit was speaking in other languages, but that the individuals were speaking in other languages and that they were enabled to do this by the help of the Spirit. So the narrative provides a description of cooperation between each individual and the Spirit. Here is a pattern that will be repeated later. People are empowered by the Spirit to do what they could not otherwise or previously do.

The chapter continues by telling us that Jerusalem was full of visitors for the celebration of the Pentecostal feast. As a Jewish festival, it marked the spring harvest and the giving of the Mosaic law. God-fearing Jews from all over the Roman world had converged on the city and were thronging the streets in preparation for a visit to the ceremonies due to take place at the Temple. The room where the followers of Jesus were speaking would not have had glass windows. Their voices floated out to the crowds below. Each person outside could recognize his or her own native language being spoken. They came from all over the Middle East and the eastern Mediterranean and were astonished at the polyglot hubbub of voices they could hear. The voices were calling out in praise to God. The crowd came to a standstill and the people in the house came outside, still speaking in tongues. Despite calling out in praise to God, they were obviously behaving in a peculiar way so that some of the crowd began to make fun and say 'they have had too much wine'. This, again, has become a thread running through Pentecostalism. Apparently inappropriate behaviour has been attributed by Pentecostals to the overwhelming power of the Spirit.

The narrative of Acts continues:

> Then Peter stood up with the Eleven, raised his voice and addressed the crowd: 'Fellow Jews and all of you who live in Jerusalem, let me explain this to you; listen carefully to what I say.
>
> These men are not drunk, as you suppose. It's only nine in the morning! No, this is what was spoken by the prophet Joel:
>
> "In the last days, God says, I will pour out my Spirit on all people. Your sons and daughters will prophesy, your young men will see visions, your old men will dream dreams. Even on my servants, both men and women, I will pour out my Spirit in those days, and they will prophesy"...Jesus of Nazareth was a man accredited by God among you by miracles...[he was] put to death....But God raised him from the dead.'

The religious experience and multilingual adventures of the believers lead straight to street preaching. The believers, led by Peter, make a public declaration about Jesus Christ in the hostile streets of Jerusalem. Despite the peculiarity of their behaviour earlier, the believers who have been filled with the Spirit have a cogent message to impart. The message is certainly centred on Christ, but it has an eschatological (end-of-time) dimension. Peter tells the crowd that what they are witnessing is the fulfilment of an ancient prophetic promise that 'in the last days' God will pour out his Spirit on all people. This motif of a universal outpouring of the Spirit is integral to Pentecostalism's understanding of its purpose. The promised outpouring of the Spirit is geographically universal and socially inclusive and intended to allow people all over the world to see visions and dream dreams, marks of prophetic inspiration in Jewish understanding. This empowerment is going to be closely linked to the story of Jesus.

Standing back from Acts 2, it is easy to see that religious experience and religious doctrine are interconnected. The experience is subjective, transitory, and unique to each participant, even if the experience occurs in a collective setting. Yet, according to the biblical text, the experience is associated with a certain kind of behaviour (speaking with tongues). It takes only a short logical leap to argue that the behaviour (speaking with tongues) is so integral to the experience that neither can occur without the other. This becomes a doctrine (something taught). How do you know that somebody has been filled by the Holy Spirit? Because they speak with other tongues. That is the conclusion, as we shall see, that many Pentecostals drew.

Behind this looms the larger question of the relationship between belief and experience. There appear to be three simple positions that can be adopted. First, belief can function more or less independently of experience, either because the belief is not obviously testable by experience (what evidence would we need to disprove the existence of angels?) or because a belief is held tenaciously in the face of experience to the contrary. Second, belief can be modified by experience so that all the time fresh experiences generate fresh beliefs. Belief is in this instance variable and constantly revised. Third, belief and experience can interact with each other so that, on some occasions, belief conforms to experience and, on other occasions, belief is primary and either informs the interpretation of experience or else shapes experience in some other fundamental way. The majority of Pentecostals (as Chapters 5 and 6 show) tended to this third position and slowly adapted to changing cultures and situations.

The dialectic between belief and experience was expressed in a series of almost forgotten proto-Pentecostal groups that appeared sporadically during the twists and turns of Christian history. The groups, inspired by their fervent spiritual experiences, characteristically railed against fixed beliefs and immoveable institutional forms, and this was later to give rise to the amorphous character of Pentecostalism with its thousands of denominations.

Spirit and institution

In the mid-2nd century, after the first creative surge of Christianity had been completed, a new movement began in Phrygia in modern-day Turkey. Montanus, a pagan priest of Cybele, was converted to Christianity and began to prophesy. He predicted that the return of Christ would occur near where he lived and anticipated a new age of the Spirit ushered in under his own prophetic leadership. His utterances were given in the first person singular as if directly from the Holy Spirit, and he was soon joined by two women, Maximilla and Priscilla, who deserted their husbands with Montanus's approval and added their voices to his prophetic ministry. Declaring that the existing church was too soft and inclusive, they urged higher levels of asceticism, fasting, and abstinence from marriage. They also attacked the church for the absence of spiritual gifts and demanded their own prophecies be given a status above that of the canonical Scriptures. Not surprisingly, Montanism provoked opposition, which eventually stamped it out, but its influence lingered on in parts of Asia and North Africa for at least another 400 years.

A long line of Christian mystics in the medieval period managed, for the most part, to remain on good terms with mainstream Christianity by being situated within religious orders. Julian of Norwich (c. 1342–c. 1416), for instance, lived as a hermit in a cell attached to the side of the church and wrote eloquently about her revelation of the bleeding head of Christ and the inner relations within the Trinity and the influence of the Spirit in prayer. Thomas Müntzer (1488–1525), on the other hand, showed how religious experience purportedly inspired by the Holy Spirit could lead to violent civil disorder. Beginning as a disciple of Luther but soon becoming more radical still, Müntzer came to believe that an inner baptism by the Spirit eclipsed all conventional religious rites. Expounding the idea that the inner light imparted by this baptism superseded the authority of Scripture, and confident that he could distinguish between revelations flowing from God and those of devilish spirits, Müntzer declared the righteous should use their swords to fulfil the will of God by establishing the kingdom of God upon earth. The Peasants' War followed, but the radical left wing of the Reformation was crushed by military force and Müntzer was captured, tortured, and beheaded.

More enduring and more peaceful was Pietism, which emerged in the Lutheran churches in the late 17th and early 18th centuries. This was an introspective, unworldly, and prayerful renewal movement that valued Bible reading, spiritual experience, and charitable activity without attempting major ecclesiastical or social reform. Through the Moravians, Pietism made an impact on the Wesley brothers.

Methodism and after

John and Charles Wesley were the sons of an Anglican clergyman and an ardent spiritually disciplined mother. During their childhood, the family home was set on fire and John was rescued from an upstairs window in the nick of time. Thereafter, John believed that his life had been saved for a divine purpose. He grew up as a highly organized, intelligent, priggish young man who, while at Oxford, took over leadership of a club that methodically (hence 'Methodism') pursued a round of Bible study, prison visiting, prayer, and academic work. Travelling to the American colonies to preach, John had little success and returned home disappointed. On the Atlantic voyage, he had observed a group of Moravians at close hand and marvelled at their calmness during a storm; while everyone else panicked, they sang hymns. In 1738, at a meeting in London, a Moravian pastor was reading aloud from Luther's writings and John reported,

> while he was describing the change which God works in the heart through faith in Christ, I felt my heart strangely warmed. I felt I did trust in Christ, Christ alone, for salvation; and an assurance was given me that He had taken away my sins, even mine.

This evangelical conversion (or 'new birth') focusing upon trust in Christ became the hallmark of Methodist preaching. It was a preaching that aimed at the heart for an emotional response. This led to a doctrine of 'assurance', or the intellectual conviction based on spiritual experience that sin had been removed by God. This, in short, was a preaching that could coordinate emotion and reason in a powerful synthesis.

For more than 50 years, John Wesley (1703–91) travelled round Britain and the United States preaching. It is estimated that he covered 250,000 miles on horseback as he rode from town to town ('the world is my parish'). Typically, he would preach three times a day and, as the number of converts grew, he organized them into mutually supporting groups, or 'classes', which, at first, were designed to function alongside Anglican parishes and congregations. With an astonishing industriousness, Wesley wrote numerous sermons, prayers, instructional manuals, and hymns and preached in the open air, sometimes to as many as 20,000 people. His plain words, which usually stressed the importance of an individual response to his message ('O let me commend my saviour to you'), resulted in tears or, on many occasions, paroxysms of repentant grief and cries for mercy. Methodism, for all its organizational efficiency and narrow self-discipline, had an emotional drive that was captured in its hymn singing and expressed in its love feasts. Charles wrote an estimated 9,000 hymns, and the brothers published 30 hymnals over the years, often organizing material to reflect the Christian life as they saw it: the atonement of Christ, the invitation to believe, salvation, being holy, sharing the faith with others, perseverance, death, and heaven. The love feasts, social gatherings with a little food where anyone could say something, enabled people to take their first steps in public speaking while creating a sense of community more intimate than that fostered by a formal church service.

After John Wesley's death, Methodism continued to grow, though it subdivided into several theological and organizational variants. It caught the wave of national expansion westward in the United States so that by 1840 Methodists were the largest religious group in America. For every six Baptists, there were now ten Methodists, and Methodists outnumbered the combined membership of Presbyterian, Congregational, Episcopal, Lutheran, and Reformed churches by a similar ratio. In Europe, the results were less startling, though Methodism's ability to reach into the urban heartland generated by the Industrial Revolution was significant. Elsewhere, Methodism expanded along trade routes, by which it reached the West Indies, Canada, southern and West Africa, Ceylon (now Sri Lanka), southern India, and Australasia. From North America, by the 1890s it had moved southward to Mexico, Brazil, Uruguay, Venezuela, Bolivia, and Chile. Wherever Methodism went, Pentecostalism would later follow.

North American Methodism arranged summer camps where circuit preachers achieved an intensity not possible during the normal domestic rota of services. In 1801, Cane Ridge in Kentucky saw exuberant scenes full of 'godly hysteria', wild dances, 'holy laughter', and such phenomena as jerking and falling over. Such behaviour had been part of the American religious repertoire since the revivals under Jonathan Edwards (1703–58), but what was different about this was that it took place within an Arminian theological framework. Unlike the Puritan Edwards, whose theology was Calvinistic, Wesley emphasized the importance of human free will and this partly explains the tenor of his preaching as well as the frenetic activity of his life. Wesley believed that conversion or justification after initial faith in Christ would be followed by a long period of sanctification (becoming increasingly free of personal sin until inbred sin was removed). This produced a two-stage pattern, each stage of which was marked by an appropriate experience. Moreover, Wesley had read the philosopher John Locke and appreciated the argument that 'all the knowledge we naturally have is originally derived from our senses'. It follows that sense experience trumps speculative theology or philosophy.

The process of sanctification might well involve peaks or crises. John Fletcher (1729–85) had been Wesley's designated successor until Wesley outlived him. Fletcher connected a crisis experience of sanctification with baptism in the Holy Spirit as described in the Book of Acts. There is disagreement about the extent to which Wesley identified with Fletcher's position but, from the point of view of the eventual appearance of Pentecostalism, the connection between Wesleyan sanctification and baptism in the Holy Spirit is highly significant. The term 'baptism in the Holy Spirit' is crucial to later Pentecostal theology. In addition, the Wesleyan doctrinal template of justification and sanctification, both of which had experiential dimensions, was well suited to the establishment of a theology which was to highlight the role of the Holy Spirit in the Christian life.

Eschatology

The Bible contains many prophecies and promises. The Old Testament promises largely concern the status of Israel. The

New Testament promises largely concern the return of Christ. Mathematically inclined Christians who accepted the accuracy of the Scriptures could exert their ingenuity to calculate the sequence of future events. Those who took a less precise view of the biblical text might still be guided by a broad conception of the direction of history. For the sake of simplicity, it is easiest to divide general expectations into two kinds: optimistic ones which presume an upward path towards peace and harmony culminating in the kingdom of God, and pessimistic ones full of cataclysms that are only ended by the return of Christ, the judgement of sinners, and culminating in the divine kingdom.

Conferences held at Albury Court, Surrey, England, between 1826 and 1830 drew clergy and laity from the evangelical wing of the Church of England and the Church of Scotland, together with representatives of the Free Churches. The conferences ended with all the participants agreeing that the Jews would soon be converted and after this Christ himself would come back. Among those attending these conferences was a Scottish minister, Edward Irving (1792–1834), who believed that, in addition to the restoration of the Jewish people to their homeland, the church would be restored to its early glory through the renewed miraculous activity of the Holy Spirit. Irving preached in London to large and fashionable crowds until an outbreak of glossolalia (speaking with tongues) occurred in his congregation. When the Church of Scotland arraigned him, he left to found the Catholic Apostolic Church which, after his death from tuberculosis in 1834, lapsed. This is the first glimmering of Pentecostalism in the modern era. It lingered on, and the threat to the world order is mentioned by Winston Churchill in his autobiography, *My Early Life*: the sombre prophecies of 'Irvingite religion' spoke of cataclysms to come.

Among those who were influenced by Albury was John Nelson Darby (1800–82), who had trained as an Anglican priest, and who offered a novel interpretation of what the Bible said about the future. He managed to combine the optimistic and pessimistic elements within Scripture by assuming that the return of Christ would take place in two phases. In the first, Christ would return invisibly to 'rapture' (or seize) his church, leaving behind the rest of humanity to face the terrors of the Antichrist. The Jewish people would undergo purificatory sufferings before Christ returned with his church to fight a decisive battle at Armageddon. Once the Antichrist had been defeated in this military conflict, Christ would set up his earthly reign for a thousand years.

Darby made half a dozen trips to North America after the 1850s and founded Christian Brethren congregations which propagated his end-time views. Moreover, these views were elaborated and publicized in a series of annual conferences at Niagara which ran from 1875 to 1900. Leading evangelical figures, including the preacher and publisher D. L. Moody (1837–99), took up Darby's interpretation of Scripture. This interpretation was further reinforced by the built-in commentary within the Scofield Reference Bible, first published in 1909. Once the premillennial rapture of the church became normative doctrine, there was bound to be a discernible effect upon the evangelical tradition. Every negative event might be an indication of the impending arrival of the Antichrist. Every great shake-up of the international order seemed to imply the coming of a new age. Christians had to be ready to play their part in these momentous historical events. It hardly needs to be said that the bloodshed of the 1914–18 war and preparations for the establishment of the state of Israel only appeared to confirm Darby's scheme.

Healing

Any belief in the immediate activity of the Holy Spirit could quickly be translated into a belief about healing. If the Holy Spirit could purify the heart and mind, then an extension of this power could heal the body.

For evangelistic preachers who proclaimed that forgiveness of sin was freely available as a result of the death of Christ, it was a short step to proclaim that, on the same basis, physical healing was also available. 'Jesus can heal your body as easily as he can forgive your sins.' In this way, healing moved into the public arena and became part of the standard message of itinerant proto-Pentecostal evangelists like Maria Woodworth-Etter (1844–1924). But the greatest impact was made by the confrontational and high-profile figure of John Alexander Dowie (1847–1907), who, after being educated in theology at the University of Edinburgh, ministered first in Australia and then in the United States. Dowie was a complete dualist. Sickness comes from the devil and healing comes from God, and anybody who believed in God should have nothing to do with medicine. Dowie's impact was multiplied by his daring plan to build Zion City on 6,500 acres in the Chicago area. The city was to be without drugs, doctors, hospitals, saloons, dance halls, or tobacco and, according to his vision, a series of Zions would be built throughout the world, from each of which preachers would be sent out to convert the vicinity. Dowie lost credibility when, in 1901, he revealed to his perplexed followers that he was the third and final manifestation of the prophet Elijah the Restorer and when, in 1904, he claimed to be the first Apostle of the Lord Jesus Christ in the Christian Catholic Apostolic Church in Zion. A year later, he was incapacitated by a stroke and his deputy Wilbur Glenn Voliva removed him from office. Dowie died in 1907, but his uncompromising doctrine lived on among some of those who became Pentecostals.

Holiness and the Welsh revival

The Methodist Church in the United States became, in the 50 years after John Wesley's death, more staid and less evangelical. Its zeal cooled and the boisterous behaviour of its former revivalism became an embarrassing memory. Attempts to retain the early energy evolved into the debates over holiness. Phoebe Palmer (1807–74), in a book published in 1845, *The Way of Holiness*, argued for instant sanctification that could be achieved by a single dramatic act of personal consecration. Her critics said she offered nothing more than a 'parlour theology' because she avoided any social engagement along the lines that inspired Wesley's own philanthropy and his opposition to slavery. Nevertheless, 'holiness' became the watchword of reforming Methodists to the extent that, after the founding of the National Holiness Association in 1867 and the proliferation of camp meetings during holiday times, more and more congregations slipped their moorings from Methodism and banded together into holiness denominations. Many of these newer churches were to become Pentecostal or, by holding onto their holiness tenets to the exclusion of Pentecostal phenomena, vehement critics of Pentecostals.

There is much truth in the assertion that holiness could be expressed, as was Palmer's, by introverted quests for ever more refined spirituality or, as it had been in a life of the evangelist Charles Finney and, before him, in Wesley, as a socially reforming agenda. These two kinds of holiness might coalesce in revivals.

In the autumn of 1904, a young Welsh revivalist, Evan Roberts, began a meteoric public ministry that took him to the chapels and gospel halls of South Wales and then northward towards Liverpool and finally along the upper coast of Wales to Bangor. The meetings were reported not only by the local press but by the *Times* of London, and these reports were read internationally. The revival meetings were largely spontaneous because Roberts was more of an exhorter than an evangelist or teacher. There was singing in Welsh, public confession of sin, spontaneous prayer often lead by women or children, meetings stretching far into the night, and remarkable lifestyle reversals and outbreaks of communal cohesion. The court records for the time show that crime dropped spectacularly and, even within the coal mining industry, trade unions and management seemed to see eye to eye. Something like 100,000 people are said to have committed or recommitted their lives to Christ. The next chapter shows how the Welsh revival was directly connected with the emergence of Pentecostalism.

Conclusion

Multiple spiritual movements within the church trace themselves back to the Day of Pentecost described in the Book of Acts. Throughout church history, there have been individuals who wanted free-ranging spiritual experience more than the institutional regularities of the liturgy or the precepts of the Bible. Methodism's enormous success in the 18th and 19th centuries as well as its two-stage theology of salvation and sanctification unwittingly prepared the ground for contemporary Pentecostalism. Added to this preparatory mix was the emergence of a doctrine of healing and an impending sense of events that signalled the end of time.

Chapter 2
The United States

When it began, nobody thought to write down exactly how Pentecostalism originated; nobody realized how large Pentecostalism would become. Only later was the story of Pentecostalism constructed or reconstructed by historians. North American scholars were inclined at first to stress the importance of the Azusa Street revival in Los Angeles (see below) and to make this the focal and originating point of Pentecostalism. Later the story of Azusa Street was itself unpicked and reassessed. By contrast, European scholars early on noted the multiple origins of Pentecostalism and saw apparently spontaneous and unconnected revivals flaring up on different continents. Both sets of writers saw divine providence at work. Here was the promised global outpouring of the Spirit. Later scholars, especially those outside the tradition, remained uncommitted about exactly how Pentecostalism should be defined and how its origins should be theologically described: they were more concerned to chart the development of Pentecostalism through existing missionary organizations and to explain the growth of the movement in this way. Whether Pentecostalism had one originating centre in Azusa Street or many originating centres in different parts of the world was of more than academic interest: the essence and identity of Pentecostalism were implicated in such enquiries.

Whatever the actual place or places of origin of Pentecostalism, there is no doubt that the theology which stuck Pentecostalism together as a coordinated movement came from the United States. This theology has been known as the 'fourfold gospel' or the 'foursquare gospel' and it ascribes four roles to Jesus – Saviour, Baptizer in the Holy Spirit, Healer, and Soon-Coming King. The fourfold delineation of the gospel went back at least as far as A. B. Simpson in 1890 who, as a Bible teacher, revivalist, and founder of the Christian and Missionary Alliance, had expressed his teachings in the form of the slogan 'Christ our Saviour, Christ our Sanctifier, Christ our Healer, and Christ our Coming Lord'. Pentecostals took Simpson's words and transformed them by replacing holiness teaching on the sanctifying work of Christ with their own distinctive doctrine of baptism in (or with or by) the Holy Spirit. Even so, whatever their precise theology, the *style* of Pentecostalism was revivalistic and, though some of the unpredictable phenomena were similar to those found in old Methodist camp meetings, other elements, including the singing, clapping, and public testimony, can probably be traced back to the Afro-American slave religion on the plantations of the South.

The world before 1914

The dispersion of Pentecostalism in the period before 1914 was facilitated by four factors. First, universal primary education within most parts of Europe and North America had produced a literate population. Both in Britain as a result of the 1870 Education Act and the United States as a result of local initiatives, literacy levels climbed to about 90% by 1900. Mass-circulation newspapers were built upon mass literacy, but, as mobilization for the Great War was to show, such populations were more susceptible than previous ones to nationalistic manipulation. Less visible than the secular press was a large Christian literary subculture fed by denominational periodicals and specialist journals (for instance on eschatology). Most of these periodicals of a Protestant type presumed access to a Bible, and here the revered English of the King James Version provided a common idiom.

Second, colonial expansion at the end of the 19th century had produced a world in which 90% of the globe was controlled by European powers, all of which, even France, were 'Christian'. Britain had the lion's share of this, in the sense that the British Empire both in its landmass and in the proportion of the world's population within its borders amounted to about 25%. Holders of passports issued by colonial powers were favoured by colonial administrators. The territorial extent of the British Empire universalized the English language, an effect supplemented by the growth of North American influence.

Third, the steamship and wireless telegraphy (the first transatlantic transmission occurred in 1902) began shrinking the globe, a process whose beginnings might be dated to the founding of the Universal Postage Union in 1874. Although it was still a three-week voyage by ship from England to South Africa, the telegraph could at least convey urgent information instantly, and the extension of the banking system, allowing international transfers of money, paralleled advances in communications.

Fourth, missionary expansion during the 19th century ensured that the proportion of the world's population connected with the churches increased more rapidly than at any other time since the 4th and 5th centuries of the Common Era. Whereas in 1750 only about 22% of the world population might be called Christian, this figure had risen by 1900 to about 34%. Many missionary societies came into being after William Carey's founding of the Baptist Missionary Society in 1792. Missionary societies might be denominational in the case of large and prosperous denominations, or interdenominational. Churches in the United States, Canada, Switzerland, Great Britain, Germany, France, the Netherlands, Sweden, Norway, Denmark, and Finland all launched missions of one kind or another in this period, and in most cases the first port of call for foreign missions was their nation's colonial territory. Beyond this first step of expansion, 'faith missions', almost always of an interdenominational kind, took bold risks to reach remoter regions of the world. Foremost among these was the China Inland Mission (CIM) which, though it was never Pentecostal in character, demonstrated how missionary work could be carried out without guaranteed financial support. CIM missionaries, many of whom were British, were expected to trust God for their physical and financial needs and, more importantly for missionary strategy, made their decisions on the field itself rather than being directed from an overseas headquarters in their sending country. In the years that followed, Pentecostal missionaries eagerly, and often irresponsibly, adopted the faith principle.

Whatever damage the Civil War (1861–5) did to the psyche of the United States, the next half-century saw huge and optimistic social changes. Not only did more than 15 million people emigrate to the States between 1877 and 1910, but there was internal migration in a westward direction using the new railroads; the first coast-to-coast rail link was completed in 1869. In 1870, the urban population stood at 10 million, and in the next 30 years this figure tripled. During this time, American steel production grew to the extent that by 1914 the United States was producing more steel than the whole of Europe combined. With steel came longer bridges and taller buildings, so that iconic city skylines lit by electrification and served by public transport systems sprang up. Capitalism expressed by giant new corporations and factory-based production lines began to dominate the new landscape. Great discrepancies between poor and rich provoked labour unrest without stemming the acceleration of technological advance. Church buildings reaped the benefits of rising prosperity, particularly as many of the migrants were broadly Christian: the number of congregations increased by 130% in the years 1870–90.

In his memorably titled book, *Vision of the Disinherited*, R. M. Anderson offered an explanation of religious life in the United

States in the first part of the 20th century. The men and women who flowed into the new American cities came from an agrarian setting. They found work in mills, mines, and factories, and raised their families in low-grade tenement housing. In this harsh urban environment, the displaced population felt a yearning for the rural innocence of their childhood, and the biblical promise of Christ's return offered a blessed prospect of hope. Speaking in tongues, when it occurred – we shall see how this doctrine was developed – was an ecstatic escape into a transcendent realm.

But this explanation does not work in the Asian context, for instance for missions founded in India or in Korea. At the Mukti mission, founded and directed by the scholarly and high-caste Hindu convert to Christianity Pandita Ramabai (c. 1858–1922), a large number of orphans and widows were provided with communal accommodation, a farm, and education, first near Mumbai (Bombay) and later in Pune (Poona). Ramabai had been influenced by the Keswick Conference in England which taught 'sanctification by faith'. In 1898, she was joined by Minnie Abrams (1859–1912). Abrams was a fervent Methodist and brought a new evangelical edge to the mission. In 1905, as many as 550 of the young women, who had been engaging in daily intercessory prayer, began preaching in the local villages. By the summer, revival phenomena broke out, with reports of baptisms with the Holy Spirit. The girls identified a burning sensation with the presence of the Holy Spirit, and some began to receive visions and dreams. Several girls spoke in tongues, and the phenomena spread to South India by means of a conference sponsored by the Anglican Church Missionary Society. In 1906, Abrams wrote *The Baptism of the Holy Ghost and Fire*, a book that described the revival and outlined her restorationist theological understanding of what was taking place.

In Korea, Methodist missionaries met in 1903 for a week of Bible study on the subject of the Holy Spirit. This was followed by public confession of sin and spiritual renewal. The following year,

1. Pandita Ramabai was a converted Hindu and leader of the Mukti mission in India, where, in 1905, Pentecostal phenomena occurred in a revival that lasted at least two years

the studies were repeated and 700 converts in Pyongyang were added to the churches. In 1906, a first-hand account of the Welsh revival was given by a visiting preacher. The following year, the Korean revival attracted larger crowds, and miracles of healing were reported.

Azusa Street

The man who was central to the Azusa Street revival was the son of two freed slaves, an African-American, whose family had originally been Roman Catholic and who had made a long spiritual pilgrimage that took him through Methodism to what became a classical Pentecostal position. William J. Seymour (1870–1922) reached Los Angeles on 22 February 1906, after he had spent about six weeks at a Bible school in Houston, Texas, run by Charles Fox Parham (1873–1929). Parham had made the connection between baptism in the Holy Spirit and speaking with tongues (a connection, it must be admitted, that he probably heard from Frank Sandford whom he had visited in the summer of 1900). Tongues were the biblical sign of baptism in the Holy Spirit. This was the message that Seymour had learned from Parham, a message he defended with conviction by exposition of the New Testament. Seymour's theology envisaged a three-stage process. First, salvation by faith in Christ; second, sanctification or holiness; third, baptism in the Holy Spirit evidenced by speaking with tongues as a gift that empowered Christians for service.

Accounts agree that Seymour was a dignified and gracious man. Photographs usually show him in a formal, unsmiling pose, bearded, wearing a suit, and carrying a Bible. He was described as humble, soft-spoken, gentle, and unassuming, but this does not mean that he was a weak or ineffective leader. During the early stages of the revival, he spent many hours each day praying. All that he did was designed to bring about an interracial congregation. The leadership team of his congregation included men and women, both black and white. This ideal for the church,

2. The leadership of the Azusa Street mission was noted for its racial and gender mix. W. J. Seymour is seated in the middle

at a time when segregationist laws prevented intermarriage or integrated education, was quite exceptional, and his ideals came directly from his reading of Scripture: 'we being many are one bread, and one body' (1 Corinthians 10.17).

The city of Los Angeles was a boom town. It had doubled its population in six years and by 1906 had reached 238,000. It continued to grow at the rate of 3,000 per month, and the people who flooded in comprised a variety of ethnicities, colours, languages, and social classes. The railroad terminated at Los Angeles, with the result that there were employment opportunities, and, in addition, connecting the smart modern buildings was an efficient streetcar network that enabled the poorer people to move rapidly around the city. The religious life of the area was expressed in all kinds of churches, and there were influential newspapers that helped create a common consciousness. Yet unknown to the inhabitants, the city was built near to the San Andreas Fault which ran northward up the coast towards San Francisco.

Seymour had come to Los Angeles as the pastor of a holiness congregation but, when he began to teach that there was a separate empowering experience beyond sanctification, he ran into trouble. He was locked out of his building by the trustees and found himself unemployed. Undaunted, he began a prayer meeting and conducted Bible studies in a private home on Bonnie Brae Street. On 9 April 1906, revival phenomena broke out, including speaking and singing in tongues. Seymour's teachings were being translated into actuality. The group arranged to relocate to 312 Azusa Street in a two-storey building that had once served as an African Methodist Episcopal Church. The congregation had previously met upstairs while they tethered their horses downstairs. The building was in a state of disrepair but, nevertheless, Seymour's group began their services. A reporter of the *Los Angeles Daily Times* attended the Tuesday night meeting on the 17 April and wrote a derogatory report, published the following day under the heading 'Weird Babel of Tongues'. Whatever attention this report may have received was swept away by that morning's earthquake in San Francisco 350 miles to the north. The churches of Los Angeles were mostly unwilling to attribute the earthquake to God, but at least one freelance preacher, Frank Bartleman, could interpret the event no other way. He wrote a tract, *The Earthquake!!!*, printed at his own expense and distributed throughout the city so that by the middle of May over 125,000 copies had been circulated. Bartleman saw the earthquake in eschatological terms as a dramatic call from God to repentance. This, together with the speaking in tongues and the healings that were beginning to occur, intensified the Azusa Street meetings, which now began to run more or less continuously round the clock and reached about 1,500 people during the course of a day. Visitors from all over the city, and then the country, and finally from across the world began to attend in order to receive their own Pentecostal baptism. Approximately

3. **The simple wooden building on 312 Azusa Street, Los Angeles, where the Pentecostal revival ran from 1906 to around 1912 and from which many subsequent Pentecostal denominations can trace their origins**

one-third of those who attended were ministers or missionaries who came looking for spiritual power and the gift of tongues. Having received what they came for, these people returned to disseminate the Azusa Street message and experience. Seymour started a monthly newspaper, *The Apostolic Faith*, which rapidly reached a distribution of 50,000 copies and further publicized events and doctrines, creating fresh momentum when similar outbreaks of speaking with tongues, prophecies, visions, and miracles began to occur elsewhere.

Denominational formations in the United States

The Azusa Street revival was an independent congregation, although the name of its newspaper, *The Apostolic Faith*, was one that had been used by Parham for a group of churches in the Midwest. The fame of the revival led Seymour to be invited on preaching tours in different parts of the United States, with the

William J. Seymour (1870–1922)

Seymour's pilgrimage from Roman Catholicism to holiness Methodism to Pentecostalism speaks of the seriousness of his religious quest. Early historians of Pentecostalism tended to overemphasize the role of Charles Fox Parham and to ignore Seymour. Recent research shows Seymour to have been a rounded and a balanced leader whose disgraceful treatment by a series of white preachers who tried to take over his church tested his patient graciousness to the limits. Seymour's conception of Pentecostalism was broader than that of his contemporaries; he saw its missionary implications very early on and, equally, he believed it to be fundamentally egalitarian because the Spirit was poured out regardless of people's race or gender. His leadership was firm but unobtrusive, and the revival at Azusa Street was not as chaotic as its detractors claimed. There was organized evangelism using the new Los Angeles public transport system, a vision for a renewed and multiracial end-time church, and a robust theology of spiritual gifts (that is, healing, prophecy, and speaking in tongues). Eventually, in 1915, after revival had subsided, the Azusa Street congregation revised its constitution and vested leadership only in African-American ministers. After Seymour's death, his wife Jennie took over leadership until the building was demolished in 1931.

consequence that he was frequently away from his base. At some point in 1908, two members of his congregation moved north to Oregon and began a new and independent branch of the Apostolic Faith movement. The newspaper, together with its subscription list, moved north as well, with the result that Seymour's national influence waned. There is dispute over whether the name and subscription list were 'stolen' from the Azusa Street Mission; certainly, Seymour attempted by legal means to regain what had been lost. In the sense that congregations using the name

'Apostolic Faith' were already seeking a common identity, incipient organization was evident. Seymour continued to teach and believe that sanctification was a second, definite work of grace that necessarily preceded baptism in the Spirit, and that baptism in the Spirit was accompanied by speaking with tongues. Other denominations and independent congregations began to be influenced by Azusa Street and to amend their own basis of beliefs to include the third Pentecostal stage. Some of these groups belonged to denominations that had divided from Methodism over holiness doctrine. Some groups were governed by bishops and others by more Presbyterian principles. In short, the Azusa Street revival sent ripples through ecclesiastical polity as well as through tenets of faith.

William Durham (1873–1912), originally a Baptist, first visited the Azusa Street revival in 1907 where he spoke in tongues for the first time. Durham was a dynamic preacher and an eloquent apologist for his beliefs. His surviving writings are among the most expressive and forceful of the period. At some point in 1910, Durham revised his theology by arguing that the 'finished work' of Christ upon the cross was sufficient to secure both justification and sanctification. In this way, he compressed the first and second stages of Seymour's doctrinal scheme into one. No longer was it obligatory to undergo a prolonged period of spiritual consecration in order to reach the sanctification necessary to allow baptism in the Spirit. Rather, everything the believer needed was implicit in the original saving transaction with God.

Durham's new theology shook the proto-Pentecostal movement. If sanctification could be scrapped, what else might be removed? As Pentecostal denominations began to form, a division can be made between those that rejected Durham's views and continued to insist upon the importance of sanctification or holiness as a preliminary to empowerment by the Holy Spirit and others that did not. Moreover, the denominations that began to emerge were often divided up on racial lines, with the result that very few had

THE APOSTOLIC FAITH

"Earnestly contend for the faith which was once delivered unto the saints."—Jude 3.

Vol. 1, No. 1   Los Angeles, Cal., September, 1906   Subscription Free

Pentecost Has Come

Los Angeles Being Visited by a Revival of Bible Salvation and Pentecost as Recorded in the Book of Acts

The power of God now has this city agitated as never before. Pentecost has surely come and with it the Bible evidences are following, many being converted and sanctified and filled with the Holy Ghost, speaking in tongues as they did on the day of Pentecost. The scenes that are daily enacted in the building on Azusa street and at Missions and churches in other parts of the city are beyond description, and the real revival is only started, as God has been working with His children mostly, getting them through to Pentecost, and laying the foundation for a mighty wave of salvation among the unconverted.

The meetings are held in an old Methodist church that had been converted in part into a tenement house, leaving a large, unplastered, barn-like room on the ground floor. Here about a dozen congregated each day, holding meetings on Bonnie Brae in the evening. The writer attended a few of these meetings and being so different from anything he had seen and not hearing any speaking in tongues, he branded the teaching as third-blessing heresy and thought that settled it. It is needless to say the writer was compelled to do a great deal of apologizing and humbling himself to get right with God.

In a short time God began to manifest His power and soon the building could not contain the people. Now the meetings continue all day and into the night and the fire is kindling all over the city and surrounding towns. Proud, well-dressed preachers come in to "investigate." Soon their high heels are replaced with wonder, then conviction comes, and very often you will find them in a short time wallowing on the dirty floor, asking God to forgive them and make them as little children.

It would be impossible to state how many have been converted, sanctified and filled with the Holy Ghost. They have been and are daily going out to all points of the compass to spread this wonderful gospel.

BRO. SEYMOUR'S CALL.

Bro. W. J. Seymour has the following to say in regard to his call to this city:

"It was the divine call that brought me from Houston, Texas, to Los Angeles. The Lord put it in the heart of one of the saints in Los Angeles to write to me that she felt the Lord would have me come over here and do a work, and I came, for I felt is was the leading of the Lord. The Lord sent the means, and I came to take charge of a mission on Santa Fe Street, and one night they locked the door against me, and afterwards got Bro. Roberts, the president of the Holiness Association, to come down and settle the doctrine of the Baptism with the Holy Ghost, that it was simply sanctification. He came down and a good many holiness preachers with him, and they stated that sanctification was the baptism with the Holy Ghost. But yet they did not have the evidence of the second chapter of Acts, for when the disciples were all filled with the Holy Ghost, they spoke in tongues as the Spirit gave utterance. After the president heard me speak of what the true baptism of the Holy Ghost was, he said he wanted it too, and told me when I had received it to let him know. So I received it and let him know. The beginning of the Pentecost started in a cottage prayer meeting at 214 Bonnie Brae."

LETTER FROM BRO. PARHAM.

Bro. Chas. Parham, who is God's leader in the Apostolic Faith Movement, writes from Tonganoxie, Kansas, that he expects (D. V.) to be in Los Angeles Sept. 15. Hearing that Pentecost had come to Los Angeles, he writes, "I rejoice in God over you all, my children, though I have never seen you; but since you know the Holy Spirit's power, we are baptized by one Spirit into one body. Keep together in unity till I come, then in a grand meeting let all prepare for the outside fields I desire, unless God directs to the contrary; to meet and see all who have the full Gospel when I come."

THE OLD-TIME PENTECOST.

This work began about five years ago last January, when a company of people under the leadership of Chas. Parham, who was studying God's word, tarried for Pentecost in Topeka, Kans. After searching through the country everywhere, they had been unable to find any Christians that had the true Pentecostal power. So they laid aside all commentaries and notes and waited on the Lord, studying His word, and what they did not understand they got down before the heath and asked God to have wrought out in their hearts by the Holy Ghost. They had a prayer tower from which prayers were ascending night and day to God. After three months, a sister who had been teaching sanctification for the baptism with the Holy Ghost, one who had a sweet, loving experience and all the carnality taken out of her heart, felt the Lord lead her to have hands laid on her to receive the Pentecost. So when they prayed, the Holy Ghost came in a mighty way and she spoke in tongues. Different ones then began to seek God for the Bible evidence, and three nights afterward, twelve students received the Holy Ghost, and prophesied, and cloven tongues could be seen upon their heads. They then had an experience that measured up with the second chapter of Acts, and could understand the first chapter of Ephesians.

Now after five years something like 13,000 people have received this gospel. It is spreading everywhere, until churches who do not believe backslide and lose the experiences they have. Those who are older in this movement are stronger, and greater signs and wonders are following them.

The meetings in Los Angeles started in a cottage meeting, and the Pentecost fell there three nights. The people had nothing to do but wait on the Lord and praise Him, and they commenced speaking in tongues, as they did at Pentecost, and the Spirit sang songs through them.

The meeting was then transferred to Azusa Street, and since then multitudes have been coming. The meetings begin about ten o'clock in the morning and can hardly stop before ten or twelve at night, and sometimes two or three in the morning, because so many are seeking, and some are slain under the power of God. People are seeking three times a day at the altar and now after row of souls have to be emptied and filled with seekers. We cannot tell how many people have been saved, and sanctified, and baptized with the Holy Ghost, and healed of all manner of sicknesses. Many are speaking in new tongues, and some are on their way to the foreign fields, with the gift of the language. We are going on to get more of the power of God.

Many have laid aside their glasses and had their eye sight perfectly restored. The deaf have had their hearing restored.

A man was healed of asthma of twenty years standing. Many have been healed of heart trouble and lung trouble.

Many are saying that God has given the message that He is going to shake Los Angeles with an earthquake. First, there will be a revival to give all an opportunity to be saved. The revival is now in progress.

The Lord has given the gift of writing in unknown languages, also the gift of playing on instruments.

A little girl who walked with crutches and had tuberculosis of the bones, as the doctors declared, was healed and dropped her crutches and began to skip about the yard.

All over this city, God has been setting homes on fire and coming down and melting and saving and sanctifying and baptizing with the Holy Ghost.

Many churches have been praying for Pentecost, and Pentecost has come. The question is now, will they accept it? God has answered in a way they did not look for. He came in a humble way as of old, born in a manger.

The secular papers have been stirred and published reports against the movement, but it has only resulted in drawing hungry souls who understand that the devil would not fight a thing unless God was in it. So they have come and found it was indeed the power of God.

Jesus was too large for the synagogues. He preached outside because there was not room for him inside. This Pentecostal movement is too large to be confined in any denomination or sect. It works outside, drawing all together in one bond of love, one church, one body of Christ.

A Mohammedan, a Sudanese, by birth, a man who is an interpreter and speaks sixteen languages, who came to the meetings at Azusa Street and the Lord gave him messages which none but himself could understand. He identified, interpreted and wrote number of the languages.

A brother who had been a spiritualist medium and who was so possessed with demons that he had no rest, and was on the point of committing suicide, was instantly delivered of demon power. He then sought God for the pardon of his sins and sanctification, and is now filled with a different spirit.

A little girl about twelve years of age was sanctified in a Sunday afternoon children's meeting, and in the evening meeting she was baptized with the Holy Ghost. When she was filled from standing near remarked, "Who can doubt such a clear case of God's power."

In about an hour and a half, a young man was converted, sanctified, and baptized with the Holy Ghost, and spoke with tongues. He was also healed from consumption, so that when he visited the doctor he pronounced his lungs sound. He has received many tongues, also the gift of prophecy, and writing in a number of foreign languages, and has a call to a foreign field.

Many are the prophecies spoken in unknown tongues and many the visions that God is giving concerning His soon coming. The heathen must first receive the gospel. One prophecy given, in an unknown tongue was interpreted, "The time is short, and I am going to send out a large number in the Spirit of God to preach the full gospel in the power of the Spirit."

About 150 people in Los Angeles, more than on the day of Pentecost, have received the gift of the Holy Ghost and the Bible evidence, the gift of tongues, and many have been saved and sanctified, nobody knows how many. People are seeking at the altar three times a day and it is hard to close at night on account of seekers and those who are under the power of God.

When Pentecostal lines are struck, Pentecostal giving commences. Hundreds of dollars have been laid down for the sending of missionaries and thousands will be laid down. No collections are taken for rent, no begging for money. No man's silver or gold is coveted. The silver

to carry on His own work. He can also publish His own papers without asking for money or subscription price.

In the meetings, it is noticeable that while some in the rear are opposing and arguing, others are at the altar falling down under the power of God and feasting on the good things of God. The two spirits are always manifest, but no opposition can kill, no power to earth or hell can stop God's work, while He has consecrated instruments through which to work.

Many have received the gift of singing as well as speaking in the inspiration of the Spirit. The Lord is giving new voices, He translates old songs into new tongues, He gives the music that is being sung by the angels and has a heavenly choir all singing the same heavenly song in harmony. It is beautiful music, as instruments are needed in the meetings.

A Nazarene brother who received the baptism with the Holy Ghost in his own home in family worship, in trying to tell about it, said, "It was a baptism of love. Such abounding love! Such compassion seemed to almost kill me with its sweetness! People do not know what they are doing when they stand out against it. The devil never gave me a sweet thing, he was always trying to get me to censuring people. This baptism fills us with divine love."

The gift of languages is given with the commission, "Go ye into all the world and preach the Gospel to every creature." The Lord has given languages to the unlearned Greek, Latin, Hebrew, French, German, Italian, Chinese, Japanese, Zulu and languages of Africa, Hindu and Bengali and dialects of India, Chippewa and other languages of the Indians, Esquimaux, the deaf mute language and, in fact the Holy Ghost speaks all the languages of the world through His children.

A minister says that God showed him twenty years ago that the divine plan for missionaries was that they might receive the gift of tongues either before going to the foreign field or on the way. It should be a sign to the heathen that the message is of God. The gift of tongues can only be used as the Spirit gives utterance. It cannot be learned like the native tongue, but the Lord takes control of the organs of speech at will. It is emphatically, God's message.

During a meeting at Monrovia, a preacher who at one time had been used of God in the Pentecost Bands under Vivian Dake, but had cooled off, was reclaimed, sanctified and filled with the Holy Ghost. When the power of God came on him his eight-year-old son was kneeling behind him. The boy had previously sought and obtained a clear heart, and when the Holy Ghost fell on the father, He also fell on him and his hands began to shake and he sang in tongues.

Bro. Campbell, a Nazarene brother, 83 years of age, who has been for 53 years serving the Lord, received the baptism with the Holy Ghost and gift of tongues in his own home. His son, who was a physician, was called and came to see if he was sick, but found him only happy in the Lord. Not only old man and old woman, but boys and girls, are receiving their Pentecost. Viola Price, a little orphan colored girl eight years of age, has received the gift of tongues.

Mrs. Lucy F. Farrow, God's anointed handmaid, who came some four months ago from Houston, Texas, to Los Angeles, bringing the full Gospel, and whom God has greatly used as she laid her hands on many who have received the Pentecost and the gift of tongues, has now returned to Houston, en route to Norfolk, Va. This is her old home which she left as a girl, being sold into slavery in the south. The Lord, she feels, is now calling her back. Sister Farrow, Bro. W. J. Seymour and Bro. J. A. Warren were the three that the Lord sent from Houston as messengers of the equal numbers of blacks and whites. Seymour's original vision of racial harmony brought about by a shared experience of the Holy Spirit receded. The process of constructing denominations was resisted by many independent-minded early Pentecostals. Yet denominations were formed in the period after 1907, and most of the Pentecostal denominations in the United States can in some way or other trace themselves back to Azusa Street. Although the Church of God in its variant forms came into being in 1886 and undoubtedly experienced speaking with tongues before 1906, Azusa gave it a new framework by which to understand itself. The Church of God in Christ, the largest African-American holiness Pentecostal church, was founded in 1896 but was Pentecostalized when C. H. Mason received his Spirit-baptism through the laying on of Seymour's hands in 1906. What became the largest grouping, Assemblies of God, was formed in 1914 in Hot Springs, Arkansas, as a result of the meeting convened to bring independent preachers and congregations into collaborative unity. The Assemblies of God, as a consequence, did not have a single founding figure and organized itself around an annual conference at which all accredited ministers could speak before decisions were taken by voting. Although, at the time, scornful criticism was directed at those who began to organize the denominations, the structures that were hammered out have stood the test of time and largely preserved the wild and unstable revivalistic fire that, by 1912, had burned itself out in Azusa Street.

The new Pentecostal denominations, in their founding documentation, provided a place for baptism in the Spirit and spiritual gifts. This cherished and distinctive place for charismatic beliefs and experience sharply differentiated Pentecostals from fundamentalists, with whom they are sometimes confused. Fundamentalists almost invariably adopted dispensationalist positions that relegated miracles and experiences of the Holy Spirit to the 1st century of the Common Era. Ultimately, fundamentalists were among the sharpest critics of Pentecostalism.

After its formation, Assemblies of God came to adopt a pacifist position, which is an indication of the marginalization of Pentecostals and of the horror evoked by the 1914–18 war. The most vociferous of Pentecostals, like Frank Bartleman, denounced the profiteering of capitalistic manufacturers of armaments. Yet, the greatest test of the stability of the young Pentecostal denominations occurred when the 'new issue' erupted.

At a camp meeting in 1913 in California, a dispute arose about the correct verbal formula to be used during water baptism. This dispute broadened so as to include a discussion about the nature of the Godhead. Those who thought the 'new issue' was a fresh revelation from God, similar in its potency to Durham's, believed the Godhead was essentially modalistic. The Father, the Son, and the Spirit of Christian theology who, within the mainstream of the church, had been explicitly understood ever since the Council of Nicaea (in 325 CE) as co-equal and co-eternal Persons, were understood by those who came to be called Oneness Pentecostals as successive expressions of the same God. This debate about the unity or triunity of God resulted in a persisting schism. The great majority of Pentecostals are Trinitarian, whereas a percentage (perhaps 10%, though the figure is hard to calculate) adhere to a form of Jesus-focused Unitarianism.

The postwar era in the United States

The Azusa Street congregation had sent out numerous missionaries. Their initial belief had been that speaking with tongues would enable missionaries to communicate miraculously with other peoples without the need for formal language training. Missionaries went to India (where they caused controversy with their teaching that speaking in tongues always accompanied Spirit-baptism), Sri Lanka, Hong Kong, China, Japan, and parts of Africa. They soon found that language learning was still necessary. When the Pentecostal denominations were formed, coordinated action followed and missions departments were established. Consistent funding streams were created to support overseas workers and, because the American economy was stronger than other economies, training schools could be built, staffed, accredited, and sustained. Pentecostals were affected by the financial crises of the 1920s and the depression of the 1930s, yet, because Pentecostalism continued to grow numerically, their denominational structures and projects continued to thrive. Denominational publications multiplied, administrative offices were built, and there were even complaints that the denominational officials and Pentecostal congregations were becoming too staid and losing their fire.

Beyond the boundaries of Pentecostal denominationalism, there were independent Pentecostals. The most high profile of these was the Canadian Aimee Semple McPherson (1890–1944). Her well-publicized gospel meetings drew enormous crowds throughout the 1920s and 1930s. McPherson was a glamorous woman whose celebrity status attracted media attention, especially when she disappeared for about a month after what appeared to be a drowning accident, only to reappear claiming that she had been kidnapped. Her detractors assumed without any proof that stood up in a court of law that she had had an affair with one of her employees, but this did nothing to diminish her drawing power. Her innovative approach to evangelism and fertile mind enabled her to be one of the first Pentecostals to adopt radio broadcasting for religious means. Her Salvation Army background sensitized her to the needs of the poor, and Angelus Temple, the huge church she built in Los Angeles, did much to distribute food and shelter to the unemployed. In broadcasts, she showed an aptitude for mobilizing political support, and she was one of the first to harness anti-evolutionary sentiment in a way that foreshadowed the later campaigning of the religious right.

Although Pentecostals were initially marginalized, by the 1940s their numerical strength was sufficient to lead the National Association of Evangelicals to invite them to join. This, despite the

5. Aimee Semple McPherson was the glamorous celebrity evangelist who shone as a broadcaster, founded Angelus Temple in Los Angeles, and established the Church of the Foursquare Gospel

objections of fundamentalists, opened the way for Pentecostals to be welcomed to mainstream American Christianity and prepared the ground for later ventures into religious broadcasting.

Conclusion

The technological vitality, religious freedom, and wealth of the United States enabled Pentecostalism to cross from coast to coast, create denominations, gather resources, organize itself, and propel its message and missionaries to many parts of the world. Pentecostalism was not 'made in the USA', but it benefited from the energy and strategic location of the Azusa Street revival, especially as the revival's main leader, W. J. Seymour, preached with such conviction about baptism in the Holy Spirit.

Chapter 3
Across the world

Pentecostals see the flow of faith across the world in the 20th century as being due to the global outpouring of the Spirit. The quotation from St Peter on the Day of Pentecost says it all: 'In the last days, God says, I will pour out my Spirit on all people. Your sons and daughters will prophesy' (Acts 2.17).

Yet – and this analogy may appear too naturalistic to many Pentecostals – the spread of Pentecostalism across the world has parallels with the spread of sport. Rugby has spread from Britain to France, Italy, Argentina, Japan, Australia, New Zealand, and Oceania. Cricket has spread from Britain to New Zealand, Australia, India, Sri Lanka, Pakistan, South Africa, and the West Indies, but not to Canada, which was also part of the British Empire. Baseball has spread from the United States to Japan and Cuba, but is not found in Europe. Football (soccer) has travelled all over the world without starting in the United States until recently. The spread of each sport seems to be dependent upon a combination of favourable elements: the local climate, room on the sporting calendar, enthusiasts (some of whom will be expatriates), and no need for expensive equipment (soccer can be played on waste ground with bare feet). Pentecostalism finds space almost anywhere, generates an army of enthusiasts, and can start with almost nothing, with street preaching and a Bible study in a hired room in the poorest part of town.

Europe

The spread of Pentecostalism to Europe depended upon a number of Pentecostal preachers, who functioned like enthusiasts in the analogy above. Foremost among these was T. B. Barratt (1862–1940), whose English father had emigrated to Norway. Barratt therefore grew up bilingual in Norwegian (which helped him communicate with Scandinavians) and English. He was in charge of the Methodist Oslo City Mission and went to the United States to try to raise funds for his work. While there, he heard of the Azusa Street outpouring and received Spirit baptism with speaking in tongues. He returned to Oslo, where his revivalistic preaching quickly led to Pentecostal phenomena. Alexander Boddy (1854–1930), an Anglican clergyman with a parish in the north of England, visited Oslo, saw the scenes, compared them favourably with the Welsh revival, and invited Barratt to his parish to preach. Barratt arrived in 1907 and stayed seven weeks. By the time he had left, groups of people were speaking in tongues and Boddy decided to organize a Whitsun Convention in Sunderland in 1908, and these conventions ran annually until 1914 when the Great War put a stop to them. Barratt visited Denmark and Sweden in 1907, Finland in 1911, Russia in 1911, and Iceland in 1920. In each case, key individuals received Spirit baptism and Pentecostalism was introduced. In addition, Andrew G. Johnson, a Swedish immigrant who had been an early participant in the Azusa Street meetings, returned to a roving Pentecostal ministry in Scandinavia for two years before embarking as a missionary to China.

The spiritual climate in Scandinavia was favourable to Pentecostalism because Lutheran Pietism had for a long time been accustomed to intense prayer and occasional outbreaks of revivalistic activity. In addition, despite the prevalence of the Lutheran church and its association with the Danish and Swedish monarchies, Methodist and Baptist churches existed within a framework permitting religious freedom. One of the key leaders of

From left to right: Bro. L. Petrus (Sweden), Mrs. Barratt and the writer (Norway), Mrs. L. Bjørner and her husband (Danmark). This photo was taken some time before the division.

6. T. B. Barratt might be called the Pentecostal 'apostle to Europe'. He founded the Filadelfia congregation in Oslo and travelled extensively, spreading the message of baptism in the Spirit

Pentecostalism in Sweden, Lewi Pethrus, had been a Baptist but, on his receipt of the Spirit baptism with glossolalia, he moved in a Pentecostal direction. The first Pentecostal congregation was formed in Sweden in 1913. Similarly, in Britain there was a strong tradition of religious freedom and this, coupled with the welcome given to Pentecostalism by a clergyman within the respectable Anglican Church, provided a stable basis from which development could occur. In Germany, Pastor Paul, a Lutheran minister, visited Barratt's convention in Oslo in 1907, and this helped to begin Pentecostalism within the structures of German evangelical Protestantism where it was at first seen as a fresh expression of Pietistic spirituality.

Italy exemplified another pattern. While the Azusa Street revival was in full flow, Italian immigrants to the United States were caught up in William Durham's fiery meetings in Chicago. While some of these converts believed they were sent by the Holy Spirit as missionaries to South America, others returned to Italy. By

1913, there were two Pentecostal congregations in southern Italy, and by 1930 nearly 150 congregations.

A parallel movement resulted in the arrival of Pentecostalism in the Netherlands. Gerrit Polman, once a Salvation Army officer, had gone to the United States in 1902 and worked with Alexander Dowie. Returning to the Netherlands in 1906, he held Pentecostal meetings in Amsterdam in 1907 before linking up with the British and attending the 1908 Sunderland Convention where, for the first time, Polman spoke in tongues. The link between Boddy and Polman continued, with a visit from Boddy to Amsterdam in the autumn of that year. In the next four years, Polman, in addition to returning many times to the UK, made thirteen trips to Germany and four to Switzerland, where his previous affiliation with Dowie was appreciated by others who had had similar connections. Pentecostal meetings were held in Paris in 1909, and a couple of years later Mrs Polman was preaching in La Havre, Rheims, and Rosny.

The question facing those who had received Spirit baptism concerned the function of their experience. Should they continue as a renewal movement within their existing churches or should they break out radically and establish new denominations? Barratt was one of the first to leave the safety of Methodism and venture into Pentecostal denominationalism. Boddy remained within the Anglican Communion all his life. What sharpened the question was the deeply held conviction that pacifism was incumbent upon Pentecostal Christians. In Britain, Boddy believed the 1914–18 war to be justified, whereas the younger emerging Pentecostal leaders were inclined to pacifism and conscientious objection – for which some of them were imprisoned.

By 1924, there were three Pentecostal denominations in Britain and similar formations across northern Europe. In Germany, Pentecostalism was given a disastrous start after the police were called to unruly meetings in Kassel in 1909 and evangelicals issued a declaration from Berlin saying that Pentecostalism was 'from below' or devilish. Soviet communism clamped down on religion after 1929, and the 300 Pentecostal congregations that had been formed by then were, together with Baptists and Catholics, subject to brutalities for the next 50 years. By and large, Pentecostalism flourished in northern Europe and the largest congregations were found in Scandinavia, particularly Sweden. In the southern European Catholic heartlands, the climate was unfriendly: Pentecostalism at first made little impression, and the same hostility was apparent in Orthodox countries like Greece where religion and national identity were closely correlated. In the summer of 1939, the first pan-European Pentecostal Conference was held but, when the bombs began to fall, church life across Europe was marginalized by military conflict. Church attendance was disrupted by conscription and evangelistic activity curtailed by petrol rationing and nightly blackouts. Italian fascists persecuted most Protestants under laws that remained in force until the 1950s. German fascists treated Pentecostals as cultish. In France, the 400 or so Pentecostal congregations that had been planted in the 1930s survived but, after 1945, when European reconstruction was the order of the day, the first generation of Pentecostal believers were middle-aged and their leadership lacking in fresh ideas. In Britain, although evangelistic meetings were organized, they rarely rivalled the bigger gatherings that had been achieved in the 1930s when, for instance, Elim's George Jeffreys filled London's Royal Albert Hall regularly for Easter conventions.

In the 1960s, Pentecostals were amazed when Baptists, Methodists, Anglicans, Brethren, Salvation Army, Congregationalists, Roman Catholics, and other Christians began to speak in other tongues. This was the charismatic movement (see Chapter 5). Pentecostal phenomena which had been shunned by many mainstream churches in the 1930s began to be welcomed in the very denominations that had stood aside in derision. When the Berlin Wall fell in 1989 and Eastern Europe opened up to the

West, Pentecostals were discovered in many parts of the old Soviet empire, and when the numbers were crunched it became apparent that the charismatic movement had also burgeoned, drawing as it did from Pentecostal experience and doctrine in the creation of flourishing renewal groups and small congregations, prayer circles, home meetings, and interdenominational conferences. The simplicity and flexibility of Pentecostalism and its charismatic parallels facilitated their spread and adoption even when the religious space in society was limited. Moreover, in the era of the Soviet empire, it transpired that the Polish government had promoted Pentecostalism (and other Protestants) as a way of trying to weaken Roman Catholicism. In the Eastern Orthodox countries like Bulgaria, the space for Protestantism is tiny, though Pentecostals occupy 90% of it.

Asia

Whereas Europe is largely confined to a single landmass, Asia, in addition to the subcontinental scope of India and China, is made up of vast numbers of islands. There are over 17,000 islands comprising Indonesia, 7,000 in the Philippines, and over 3,000 in Japan. As a result, numerous ethnic and linguistic groups have evolved, multiple trading networks have been set up, and dominance of the area by a single power has never been achieved.

Christianity is believed to have arrived in 52 CE in south India with the ministry of St Thomas, one of the original disciples of Jesus – although it is also possible that Thomas only reached west India (modern Pakistan) and that it was his converts who later travelled south. Christianity in its eastern form followed the silk routes and reached China by 635 CE.

Although the British rule in India lasted less than 200 years and extended to Pakistan and Bangladesh, that period coincided with Protestant missionary expansion. The Anglican Church was also active in educational projects and in the building of churches and cathedrals. The Mukti revival occurred in central India and many of its effects spread south where the greatest concentration of Christians lay. Missionaries from Azusa Street's Apostolic Faith arrived in 1908 (G. E. Berg) and 1913 (R. F. Cook) and worked among Brethren and holiness groups until the first Pentecostal church was opened in 1919. From the 1920s, the American Assemblies of God began to make its mark on the provinces of Kerala, Tamil Nadu, Karnataka, and Andhra Pradesh. By the 1930s, Assemblies of God, with its Presbyterian-congregational style of government, and the Church of God, with its episcopal style of government, had been established, together with offshoots and Indian variants. In 1923, the Ceylon Pentecostal Mission was at work, and soon afterwards came the Indian Pentecostal Church centred in Kerala. Missionaries from the UK arrived in 1935 (L. Livesey) and worked in remote southern areas, then moved towards Coimbatore to put new ministries in place. These ministries took an indigenous Indian form in the sense that they involved congregations that supported Bible schools, tailoring schools, leper colonies, orphanages, and homes for the blind as well as other agencies, some evangelistic and others social (J. Prakasam).

While the planting of the congregations in northern India met more Hindu resistance, this did not prevent Pentecostal advance. By the 1960s, when the charismatic movement broke out, an impact was made upon Roman Catholicism in India, and in the coming decades indigenous Indian Pentecostal groups showed all the characteristics of fully fledged Pentecostal ministry, including evangelistic healing campaigns, technological sophistication, and intensive youth work associated with lively modern music.

Pentecostalism reached China in 1907. There had already been extensive Protestant missionary work in the treaty ports on the coast and inland through the agency of the China Inland Mission (founded by J. Hudson Taylor in 1865). The earliest Pentecostal arrivals from the West (T. J. and A. McIntosh, and A. and L. Garr, who had connections with Azusa Street) reached Hong Kong and began to hold meetings in the buildings used by other Protestant missionaries and then, when there was dispute over speaking in tongues, on other premises. Their interpreter was a gifted Chinese schoolteacher, Mok Lai Chi (1868–1936), who had been born into a Christian family. He interpreted for the first Pentecostal missionaries, received the Pentecostal baptism, and, as the Pentecostal missionaries returned to their countries of origin or set off on preaching tours, Mok became the effective leader of the Pentecostal work in Hong Kong and founded his own Pentecostal mission as well as a Chinese-language newspaper, *Pentecostal Truths*, that circulated widely and helped establish congregations or prayer groups elsewhere in China.

The Pentecostal work centred on Hong Kong was supplemented by new missionaries from North America and Britain. A further centre developed in Shanghai as other missionaries arrived or existing China missionaries embraced the Pentecostal experience. There may have been as many as 150 Pentecostals scattered over 30 different sites by 1915, and this figure does not include the Chinese converts, some of whom became evangelists, church elders, or itinerant sellers of Bibles.

Later arrivals with connections to Azusa Street worked in north China from 1908, and a second Chinese-language paper, *Popular Gospel Truth*, was founded (B. Berntsen) in 1912. Additionally, missionaries within the Christian and Missionary Alliance (better known as the CMA) were partially Pentecostalized and supported revivalistic forms of Christianity. When large Pentecostal denominations in the United States were organized after 1914, further funds and personnel could be sent east in response to the constant theme of missionary strategists that China represented the largest population block on the planet and that evangelization of this relatively open land was a vital element in eschatological preparation for the return of Christ. Yet it should not be thought that Pentecostalism was simply imported from America. There is also evidence of indigenous Pentecostal, or Pentecostal-type, Christianity in the fiery preaching ministry of John Sung (1901–44), a native Chinese, whose ministry of healing went well beyond the scope of his Methodist upbringing.

Nationalistic detestation of foreigners had already boiled over into the massacres associated with the Boxer Rebellion of 1901 and, though the violence was quickly quelled, diplomats and missionaries had been among its targets. Chinese Christians felt safer breaking their links with the outside world. The True Jesus Church (accepting speaking in tongues and the holiness practice of foot-washing) was founded in 1914, and the Jesus Family (which was more communitarian) in about 1927. Though missionaries stayed – and a small group of British missionaries worked in Yunnan in the west – the Communist takeover in 1949 and Mao's Cultural Revolution in 1966 were direct assaults on Christianity of all types. Missionaries were expelled as soon as Mao's power was consolidated, and Chinese Christians were either regulated by a system of licensing or driven underground into secret meetings whose discovery could lead to prolonged imprisonment. There were Pentecostals in both the licensed churches, which largely escaped persecution, and in the unlicensed churches, which did not. Moreover, the suppression of training institutions and China's international isolation created theological inflexibility and almost monastic holiness. This might be a local matter but for the fact that the total number of Chinese people affected by the Pentecostal and neo-Pentecostal movement now runs into many millions, with some estimates putting the figure at over 50 million.

Pentecostalism arrived in the island city of Singapore in 1928, brought by missionaries intending to sail to Hong Kong. It now boasts large, thriving, and prosperous multilingual neo-Pentecostal communities with outreaches into India and other parts of Asia.

Korea presents a more complicated picture. Methodist and Presbyterian missionaries arrived in the Korean peninsula in the late 19th century. Since Presbyterians practised local church self-government, new Korean congregations were usually free of missionary control. By 1900, there was a good Korean translation of the New Testament, and in 1907, largely independently of anything else that was going on in the world, a movement of confession and forgiveness broke out, led by Korean preachers pressing congregations to be open to the Holy Spirit. New converts were made and the meetings in Pyongyang laid down the pattern of early-morning prayer, congregational fervour, and a sharp rejection of ancestral Buddhism that were to become characteristic of Korean Pentecostalism. After 1910, the occupation of Korea by militaristic Japanese made the churches one of the few focal points of Korean national identity. They even issued an ineffective Declaration of Independence in 1919. The Japanese remained in charge until the atomic bomb was dropped on them and they surrendered to the Allies in 1945. Shortly afterwards, rampant Communist forces swept south from North Korea until they were pushed back by a United Nations army commanded by an American general. Korean Christians developed a dualistic mindset to cope with the switchback fortunes of a nation. Christianity, which was seen as the religion of the Americans, was welcomed by South Korea and after 1953, in the rubble of their capital city, Korean converts began the job of rebuilding the hopes and material conditions of their fellow countrymen. Among these was a young Buddhist, David Yonggi Cho, who, while dying of tuberculosis, had decided to pray to the God of the Christians. He was converted and felt himself healed in an encounter with the power of Christ. He began his church in a leaky tent bought from the American military for $50. It was to become the largest congregation in the world, with over 700,000 members.

Unlike Korea, the Philippines had known Christianity for a long time. After centuries of Catholicism, Protestantism arrived in 1898 when the United States gained control of the territory by defeating the Spanish navy. Classical Pentecostals arrived in the 1920s and these were joined by Filipinos who had first gone to the United States for education and then returned to evangelize their home country. The churches grew in the main cities and the tribal interior, though in the interior there was a greater tendency to allow animism to influence theology and ritual. World War II brought the bitter experience of Japanese military occupation, until American-led liberation in 1944. Independence followed in 1946, and the Pentecostal churches rapidly diversified and multiplied until the burgeoning charismatic movement of the 1960s gave rise to religious broadcasting with a keen political edge. Many Filipinos had remained poor because the country's wealth was concentrated in the hands of a small number of land-owning families. The vast majority of the population claimed to be Christian and of these about 20 million, or 22%, were Pentecostal of one kind or another. With their healing crusades and social action, they offered an effective critique of a political cadre accused of systematic corruption.

Oceania

Australia has Oceania's largest landmass and population. Christianity arrived with colonization in the 18th century, and Australia participated in the revivalistic and healing streams of the late 19th century. It was a personal quest for healing, though, which eventually led a 50-year-old wife and mother of five, Sarah Lancaster, to Spirit baptism. Her discovery of a pamphlet by Alexander Boddy convinced her that Pentecostal spiritual outpourings were not confined to the pages of the Bible. Newly empowered, she opened Good News Hall in 1909 to revival scenes. Touring the country with her message of the 'foursquare gospel', she broadcast her beliefs with the monthly publication of the *Good News* journal and soon established a small number of mission congregations around the nation. When the Apostolic Faith Mission from South Africa arrived in 1926, Lancaster joined up with them. Two years later, however, they re-constituted themselves as Assemblies of God in a structure that gave greater autonomy to local congregations. The early expectations of the imminent return of Christ receded and Spirit-filled congregations and denominations took a less sectarian position, particularly after the charismatic movement among non-Pentecostal groups created a pool of Christians who found it natural to flow into Pentecostal churches in the late 1960s. By the 1980s, however, the democratic polity of Pentecostal denominations was challenged by a new emphasis upon authoritative apostolic gifts that concentrated power and control among a select few, many of whom were pastors of megachurches and accountable to no one but God.

Late 19th-century revivalistic streams also created a backdrop to New Zealand Pentecostalism, but it was not until the 1920s, when the healing evangelist Smith Wigglesworth arrived, that a sufficient momentum was gained to begin the Pentecostal Church of New Zealand. The 1918 influenza epidemic left in its wake a desire for healing and the bold faith of Wigglesworth, a plumber from Bradford, England, resulted in revivalistic meetings and dramatic claims for miracles. After early splits and secession, two main Pentecostal denominations formed, Assemblies of God and the Apostolic Church, as well as independent Pentecostal groups. The churches remained small and sectarian in attitude until the charismatic movement of the 1960s. By the 1980s, Pentecostals were campaigning unsuccessfully against the reform of legislation on homosexuality. They devoted their energies into supporting two Christian political parties set up in the 1990s. Meanwhile, the charismatic movement spilled out of the traditional denominations into new religious forms and parachurch networks while creating conditions for the formation of big congregations full of young people.

Africa

Christianity reached Africa early. There is a New Testament reference to a convert from Ethiopia (Acts 8.27f) and, in the first centuries of the Christian era, countries on the North African coast were alive with Christian congregations that were only subsequently erased by Islamic incursions. Prior to this, there were ancient African civilizations as well as nomadic tribes whose religion centred on animism and ancestral spirits. Even today, it is argued that the primal African worldview is predisposed to accept Pentecostalism because both readily acknowledge the spiritual realm.

Africa's history can broadly be divided into its precolonial phase, its colonial phases, and its postcolonial period of independence. Christianity, and especially evangelical Methodism, was at work in West Africa in the precolonial phase, although malaria and other diseases made missionary work away from the coast extremely dangerous. African converts survived longer and began educational and agricultural projects. In the colonial phase, after the European powers made their 'scramble for Africa' from the 1880s onwards, the territory was divided up by geographical boundaries or lines of latitude and longitude and, in many cases, the main intention of the Europeans was to extract as much wealth from Africa as they could. In this sense, the colonial phase was a regression, lacking much of the altruism of the 18th century. Where the colonial powers went, they took their religion and replicated its configurations on African soil. Anglican cathedrals were built by the British in South Africa, Kenya, and Zimbabwe (then Rhodesia). Catholic churches were to be found where the Belgians governed in the Congo, or the Portuguese in Angola and Mozambique, or the French in Togo and areas of West Africa. Lutherans came from Germany and Switzerland. Not all the imperial powers treated their African territories in the same way, the Belgians being particularly cruel and avaricious.

During the colonial phase, there were African prophetic movements. Wade Harris (1865–1929), brought up as a Methodist, conducted an itinerant preaching ministry in West Africa until his imprisonment in 1914. During the colonial phase, missionary work continued either despite or supported by colonial governments. William Burton and James Salter travelled by river to Mwanza in the Congo in 1915, and when independence came to the area in the 1960s their mission (CEM) had created 2,100 congregations and 2,500 workers. The Apostolic Faith Mission (AFM), led by John G. Lake and Tom Hesmalhalch, which had connections with the Azusa Street Mission, began holding meetings in South Africa in 1908. The AFM, despite its troubled history, became the largest classical Pentecostal denomination in South Africa. A more purely African leadership, and one which resisted segregation, was exemplified in the preaching of the respected Zulu evangelist Nicholas Bhengu, whose tent crusades began in 1950, ran for more than 25 years, and attracted thousands of people. Alongside this, traditional missions continued and many of the main Pentecostal denominations, including those from Scandinavia, worked systematically by building stations (which doubled up as trading posts and educational/medical centres) from which village congregations could be founded.

At the end of World War II, after a wave of independence movements, one might think that Christianity would have been rejected as the religion of the colonial masters but, as it happened, Christianity was frequently seen as beneficial, even though a few African leaders, some of whom were military dictators like Idi Amin in Uganda, attacked the church with xenophobic zeal. As a result, African Pentecostalism can now be analysed into several categories. There are AICs (or African Initiated Churches) which had often originally broken free of the old missionary organizations and are founded and directed by Africans with an admixture of African spirituality alongside traditionally Christian beliefs and practices. They might go by names like 'Redeemed Gospel Church', 'Deliverance Church', 'Jesus Is Alive Ministries', 'End Time Revival Centre', and 'Prosperity Tabernacle'. Then there are Zionist-type churches in South Africa, where the term 'Zion' refers to the city near Chicago founded by Alexander Dowie. These

7. Pentecostal-style churches, some big and many small, all over sub-Saharan Africa often preach healing, prosperity, and a deliverance gospel

8. African Pentecostalism

congregations may practise dietary restrictions and healing rituals. There are Ethiopian-type churches which may have charismatic elements in them but retain ancient liturgical patterns. In addition, there are new post-1960s charismatic churches, particularly in Anglophone parts of Africa such as in Ghana and Nigeria. These churches (sometimes called 'Aladura churches') preach a powerful health and prosperity message that is focused upon the material improvement of members, obligatory tithing, a belief in spiritual warfare, and, very often, television ministries that glamorize wealth and business success. Bumper stickers publicize the message: 'Unstoppable Achievers', 'I am a

Nicholas Bhengu (1909–86)

Bhengu, sometimes known as 'the black Billy Graham', was born in Zululand, the grandson of a Zulu chief. After an early attraction to Marxism, he returned to Christianity as a young man and received Bible training in Natal and then worked as a court interpreter by virtue of his proficiency in many languages. Being inspired by a dream to bring Africa back to God, he started travelling extensively as an evangelist and would raise funds on preaching tours in the United States, Canada, England, and Norway so as to hold massively popular tent meetings in South Africa. Resisting segregation, he established more than 50 churches by 1959, and his preaching had a profound effect wherever he went. In some areas, the crime rate dropped by as much as one-third and his churches, joining the South African Assemblies of God, came to be governed by a group of apostles among whom Bhengu was one of the leaders. At his funeral, crowds of more than 20,000 people attended, and his legacy stretched beyond South Africa into Zimbabwe and other adjacent countries.

Winner', 'I am a Stranger to Failure', 'The Blessing of the Lord Makes Rich'. This type of message has an appeal to the upwardly socially mobile as well as to the poor. The pastors of the churches become rich and serve as an example of the blessing of God and of Afro-optimism to their followers. They also stand against what they perceive to be the threat of Islam and the imposition of Sharia law.

South America

Spanish *conquistadores* and Portuguese traders brought Roman Catholicism to South America in the 16th century. From Mexico to Argentina, Catholicism changed social structures and ancestral religious values.

Early Protestant encroachments occurred with pioneering Methodism, especially in Chile, where Willis Hoover (1856–1936) travelled as a missionary. There his spiritual life was revolutionized around 1906 by reading a pamphlet on baptism in the Holy Spirit by Minnie Abrams, who worked in Mukti, India. Hoover eventually left the Methodist Church and helped bring into existence the Iglesia Metodista Pentecostal, which retained its Wesleyan theology and its episcopal governance. Pentecostalism soon grew in Chile alongside, or on top of, Methodist foundations and became an important religious force. While Catholicism criticized the dictatorial regime of Pinochet, Pentecostal bishops were drawn into giving him legitimacy – though others risked imprisonment by making their opposition plain.

In Brazil, which became home to the largest number of Pentecostals in the world, the movement began with the arrival in 1910 of two Swedish-American preachers, Daniel Berg and Gunnar Vingren, who travelled down from Chicago but who drew on valuable financial and other support from the thriving

9. Minnie Abrams was originally an evangelistic Methodist

Pentecostal churches of Scandinavia. Here, building on or standing in opposition to Roman Catholicism, Pentecostals rapidly grew. The most obvious reasons for this were to be found in the willingness of Brazilian Pentecostals to conduct their services in the Portuguese language, to allow local pastors great discretion in the running of their churches and because the message of Christ's power was effective against the endemic spiritism of Brazilian society. We may say that Pentecostalism grew 'from below' rather than being imposed in a 'top-down' way. When Pentecostals began to organize themselves to maximize their political power, they were able to win seats in government and, though they were caught up in occasional financial scandals themselves, most Pentecostals cast their votes on the basis of the perceived financial probity of candidates rather than for a political programme.

A similar engagement with politics was found among Colombian Pentecostals, though, in this case, the arrival of Pentecostalism waited until the 1930s; among its first missionaries were Oneness Pentecostals who failed to find affinity with the Trinitarians. Colombia's drug industry undermined its economy and threatened the democratic agencies of the state. Kidnappings and murders were rife, and so churches built strong protective structures, usually of a cellular kind, to resist social dislocation. Each church member belonged to a small cell, a device intended to promote discipleship and close support for threatened individuals in an unstable social order. Even so, there were Pentecostals at the very top of society serving as senators and offering support to beleaguered government officials.

In Mexico, which had long-standing military arguments with the United States, Hispanics were part of the original Azusa Street revival before they returned home and started working within a culture that was closely controlled by Catholicism. Only in 1936 was legislation enacted to enable Protestants to evangelize, and Francisco Olazábal's ministry to Mexican migrant workers in the United States and within Mexico gave additional confidence and strength to emerging Hispanic Pentecostalism. When, in the 1970s, charismatic Christians or neo-Pentecostals joined with the original classical pioneers, their combined strength made a difference to the religious life of the nation.

10. Francisco Olazábal: a powerful Hispanic preacher with a lasting legacy

In the south of the continent, Argentina opened to Pentecostal evangelism after 1909, when a Canadian, Alice Wood, brought the Pentecostal message. Italian and Danish Pentecostals joined her, with relatively minor success, until in 1954 Tommy Hicks preached a great revival crusade which, it is said, the Peróns supported. Later, after dictatorial government and the death or jailing without trial of up to 30,000 people, the defeat of General Galtieri by the British Navy led to national soul-searching and spiritual renewal that benefited the whole Pentecostal and charismatic community.

Francisco Olazábal (1886-1937)

Olazábal was born in Mexico to a pious Catholic family with traditional beliefs in saints and miracles. When he was 12 years old, his mother converted to evangelical Protestantism and became a Methodist lay evangelist. Olazábal soon found himself in Methodist ministry and conducted small-scale evangelistic campaigns in Mexico and across the border in Texas. He studied at the Moody Bible Institute and then left to work with the growing Mexican population in Los Angeles. On being persuaded that Spirit baptism was a reality, he left Methodism and joined the new and disorganized Pentecostals, working first with the Assemblies of God and then, because the American missionaries were reluctant to let the Mexican congregations govern themselves, on his own. He helped establish the Interdenominational Mexican Council of Christian Churches that, by 1924, included 34 congregations straddling the border. During the 1920s, Olazábal's ministry stepped up a gear. He travelled widely across the United States preaching to migrant workers and then, in 1931, to Spanish Harlem in New York, where about 100,000 people attended, healings took place, and men and women came to commit their lives to Christ. News of these services spread through the impoverished Italian and Anglo communities, with the result that invitations flowed in from further afield. Olazábal conducted mass evangelistic meetings in Puerto Rico in 1934 and then in Texas, before he died in a car accident on his way to an ordination service in Mexico. Olazábal is credited with contributing to the foundation of at least 14 denominations and in raising the self-respect of Latinos and their confidence in Pentecostal spirituality.

Conclusion

Pentecostalism expanded globally through missionary agencies and by the planting of self-sustaining congregations adapted to local culture. It was less welcome in Europe, where most of the larger traditional churches rejected it, but, eventually, it established a foothold in a scattering of the smaller non-liturgical Protestant churches and societies.

Chapter 4
Glossolalia, healing, prosperity, and spiritual warfare

Pentecostal theology exists at three levels. 'Ordinary theology' is
the theology of the men, women, and children who attend
Pentecostal congregations. This theology is unsystematic,
personal, and practical. It is the theology of the everyday believer
without formal theological training whose beliefs are formed out
of personal Bible reading, the sermons of the local pastor, and
religious experience. At some distance removed from this theology
is the theology of ministers who have received a seminary
education, and some distance further away again is the theology of
those who work in educational institutions and whose orientation
is likely to be academic, technical, professional, and abstract.
These three levels – represented by the person in the pew, the
minister, and the academic theologian – are by no means
necessarily in conflict with each other. Indeed, it may be that the
three levels are identical, in that the academic version merely
expresses in a more sophisticated way what ministers and church
members believe. Even so, the academic theologian and, to some
extent, the minister are likely to have an understanding of the
historical origin and development of the theological position that
they hold and, if they have travelled or read widely, an
understanding of the cultural diversity that shapes Pentecostal
beliefs in different parts of the world.

Origins

John Wesley's doctrine of sanctification (Chapter 1) provided a template for post-conversion religious experience. That this experience might be called 'baptism in the Holy Spirit' prepared the way for later Pentecostal theology. Charles Fox Parham's belief, based upon a reading of the Book of Acts, that speaking with tongues, or glossolalia, was the sign of baptism in the Spirit (Chapter 2) brought together a specific physical manifestation and a biblical religious experience. Although subsequent exegetes criticized Parham and, indeed, Pentecostal denominations that accepted his conclusions, the identification of glossolalia as a sign of Spirit-baptism had one unmistakable advantage: no longer were wild or vague appeals to feelings or prostrations required to indicate reception of the Holy Spirit. The criterion of speaking with tongues reduced the range of revivalistic phenomena that congregations or preachers were looking for in their quest for spiritual power or holiness. Doctrinal precision, in other words, gave order to the revivalistic fringes of Methodism and its holiness offshoots.

'Holiness' was a battle cry for sections of the Methodist or Methodist-related congregations in the United States, and a similar call for 'higher life' was heard through the Keswick movement in Britain that started in 1875. In effect, as evangelical congregations became prosperous and bourgeois, the concept of holiness was invoked to elicit greater dedication and more fervour. The advantage of this rallying cry was that it did not, at first, appear to require denominational reform or doctrinal adjustment. It was a call to renewal and could be stirred up in meetings at summer camps where preachers were given time to expound biblical passages at length and in detail. The consequence of this movement was to produce, at first, holiness associations and then, eventually and after painful schism, holiness denominations. When the call for holiness was linked with baptism in the Spirit, the ground for the Pentecostal revival was laid.

By the early 20th century, there were two relevant doctrinal schemes in circulation. The first presumed that baptism in the Holy Spirit followed a definite experience of holiness (or sanctification). In this scheme, only those who had already secured 'heart holiness' might find their way through to the crowning glory of Spirit-baptism. The second, largely as a result of the preaching of William Durham (1873–1912), argued that conversion ('new birth') and sanctification were both secured at once by faith in Christ. Conversion was a 'finished work' that needed no lengthy process of sanctification added to it. Baptism in the Spirit, in this scheme, became a post-conversion enduement with spiritual power for the purpose of Christian service.

A separate line of doctrinal development had focused upon physical healing. The earliest examples of this occurred through Dorothy Trudel, whose healing homes in Switzerland seem to have functioned like guesthouses for those who were ill. People could stay in these homes while they recovered from illness and at regular intervals prayer services would be held. The atmosphere appeared calm and the movement was not associated with evangelism. By 1880, Charles Cullis, a physician who had visited Trudel, began to emulate her work in the Boston area of the United States. He was already within the holiness tradition and publicized his work through *Faith Cures* in 1879. A year later, he was followed by Carrie Judd Montgomery, whose book *The Prayer of Faith* also associated healing with prayer. The biblical text that both expounded was James 5.14,15:

> Is any one of you sick? He should call the elders of the church to pray over him and anoint him with oil in the name of the Lord. And the prayer offered in faith will make the sick person well; the Lord will raise him up.

The text envisages prayer taking place within the community of the local church. The person who is ill calls for the 'elders', and they come to pray for him or her after anointing with oil. The oil, as Pentecostals subsequently came to believe, symbolized the Holy Spirit.

When healing was exegetically connected with the atonement (the crucifixion) through a reading of Isaiah 53.4, 5 and Matthew 8.17, the scene was set for healing evangelists to proclaim their message in the public arena.

Jesus

And the message the evangelists proclaimed was about Jesus. Although Pentecostals have been accused of being Spirit-centred, it is more accurate to see them as Christ-centred. Their early theology was organized around Christ as the Saviour, Healer, Baptizer in the Spirit, and Soon-Coming King. Those Pentecostals with Wesleyan roots who retained sanctification as a stage in Christian initiation also emphasized Christ as Sanctifier and so expanded the fourfold pattern into a fivefold one. But the point of these theological configurations was that they put the person and work of Jesus at the forefront of the mind of believers. In preaching of Jesus as a Saviour, Pentecostals followed exactly along the line taken by evangelicals in the past. Christ was the one who died for human sin and, in a divinely arranged substitution, took the sins and punishment that were due to every individual who ever lived. Such an act of self-sacrifice was expressed in the words of Paul, 'God demonstrates his own love for us in this: while we were still sinners, Christ died for us' (Romans 5.6), and the response, again in the words of Paul, 'I live by faith in the Son of God, who loved me and gave himself for me' (Galatians 2.20). Without understanding the message that Pentecostals preached of the love of Christ, it is impossible to understand the success of their mission. In whatever circumstances, however bad the actions of the sinner, and however old or young the sinner might be, Christ is existentially there to make a change to one's life here and now and today.

More than this, as the healing evangelists on television and in vast meetings would declare, Jesus took human illness in himself on the cross in the same way that he took human sin. In this formulation, human beings should be able to find healing by their faith in the substitutionary sufferings of Christ. This location of healing within the atonement was strongly held by many preachers and by some church members but tended to be queried by Pentecostal academics. Among other criticisms of the doctrine was the difficulty of answering the questions of men and women who sincerely believed that Christ had carried their sicknesses but who, despite every prayer, remained unmistakably ill. In its most extreme form, this doctrine resulted in a refusal to accept medical means of healing, and it was for this reason that a significant number of Pentecostal missionaries in the early part of the 20th century died of malaria and other tropical diseases. Other Pentecostals took a more balanced position, believing that, although healing might be ultimately and indirectly in the atonement, there was no contradiction between their faith and the belief that medical science should be welcomed as a blessing in its own right.

In any event, the Christ who died for the sinner was also the Christ who gave the Holy Spirit to the church. Part of the generosity of God is seen in the dispensation of the Spirit to the undeserving church. This might be put in terms of 'the blessing of Abraham' (Galatians 3.14) or in terms of Luke-Acts, where the Spirit is 'the promise of the Father' (Acts 1.4). This might also be seen in Johannine terms by reference to John chapter 14, where Jesus promises that he will send 'another comforter' (or to use the Greek word, *Paracletos*) who will be with the disciples forever. They will not be orphans when Jesus leaves them, but the Spirit will make the presence of Christ real to them in their difficult and adventurous lives (John 14.18). In their reference to Luke-Acts, Pentecostals took note of the words of Peter on the Day of Pentecost that the Spirit was poured out upon the church – and indeed the world – having been given by God to the risen Christ.

In this way, the outpouring of the Spirit is also a guarantee of the reality of the resurrection of Christ. But it is, in another sense, the bringing of the presence of Christ into the heart of the church.

By looking closely at the transition from the Gospels to the early church, and especially by looking at Acts, Pentecostals saw paradigms for the relationship between Christ and the Spirit and the Spirit and the church. Though they were accused of deriving their theology from too narrow a range of biblical data, they answered by showing how Acts could also be a source of Christian doctrine. They believed that the experiences and activities of the apostolic church were to be correlated with the more obviously doctrinal elements of Pauline epistles so that, between Acts and the epistles, there should be a perfect fit. Academic Pentecostal theologians might acknowledge that the theology of Luke (as the writer of Acts) might differ from the theology of Paul (as the writer of epistles), but most Pentecostal preachers believed that the inspiration of the Holy Spirit underlay all parts of the New Testament, with the result that there should be no contradiction between the various texts.

The Christ of the New Testament was, as Pentecostals pointed out, the one who baptized with the Holy Spirit (Matthew 3.11, Mark 1.8, Luke 3.16, John 1.33). They saw Christ as the one who administered Spirit-baptism in the same way as John the Baptist had administered water baptism. The Spirit was the element into which the believer was plunged with the result that the one who was baptized in the Spirit was completely surrounded and overwhelmed by the presence of the divine. Consequently, a specific religious experience was integral to Pentecostal identity.

The Christ who administered the Holy Spirit was also, according to the Gospels, the Christ upon whom the Spirit rested (John 1.32). While Christ himself could not be said to have been baptized in the Spirit – and he is certainly not reported as speaking in other tongues – he was, according to the New

Testament, 'anointed' with the Spirit (Acts 10.38). This anointing put him in a long line of biblical prophets and kings who had all, at one point or another in Israel's history, received an experience of the Spirit to prepare for the work they would do (e.g. 1 Samuel 16.13, Numbers 11.29, Judges 6.34). The sharp question for Pentecostals concerns the source of the miraculous power available to Christ. For some Pentecostals, the power of Christ to perform miracles depended entirely upon his reception of the Holy Spirit. It did not depend upon his inherent deity. As Edward Irving had argued in the 19th century, the Christ who came into the world emptied himself of his divine attributes (Philippians 2) and only after his baptism in the River Jordan was he empowered by the Spirit. This meant that believers in Christ who received the same Spirit might also expect the same power. Or, to put this in more formal theological language, the miraculous power of Christ derived from a Spirit Christology rather than a logos Christology. The result of this understanding was to emphasize the humanity of Christ even as it brought into focus more clearly the importance of the Holy Spirit to the portrait of Christ displayed in the Gospels.

A different perspective on the nature of Christ came from Oneness Pentecostals. This grouping had originally split off from the Trinitarian Pentecostals in 1916 after the formation of the Assemblies of God, the largest Pentecostal denomination in the United States. Oneness Pentecostals noted that the apostles in Acts baptized new believers 'in the name of Jesus' (Acts 2.38) and that this mode of baptism appears to contradict the Trinitarian formula for baptism 'in the name of the Father and of the Son and of the Holy Spirit' given in Matthew 28.19. They reconciled the two baptismal formulae by arguing that 'the name of Jesus' must be equated with the Trinitarian formula, with the result that the name of Jesus must include the Father and the Spirit. In short, they argued that the Father, Son, and Holy Spirit have been manifested to secure the salvation of human beings but, in heaven, God is revealed solely in the person of Jesus Christ, and that the

Holy Spirit is the spirit that was in Jesus Christ; there are no divisions within God's being. This does not mean that Jesus failed to become fully human but rather emphasizes the unity of the Godhead to the extent that the differentiation of divine Persons is nullified. In addition to these beliefs, Oneness Pentecostals believe that baptism in the Spirit occurs at conversion and that speaking in tongues as well as water baptism are necessary for salvation.

Contextual variants

Pentecostalism's openness to religious experience has facilitated its malleability. It is culturally relevant in the many regions where it is present, and the implication of this is that it has adapted to local situations and offered answers to local problems which are later, in the inter-communication within the Pentecostal community across the world, transferred elsewhere.

Prosperity and the Word of Faith

The earliest Christians were noted for their poverty and a renunciation of fame and fortune. Some went into the desert and lived as hermits, and others became mendicant friars walking the world as holy beggars. Prosperity teaching takes an exactly opposite position. The 'prosperity gospel' insists that it is the will of God for Christians to be wealthy and that such success is indicative of God's blessing. The prosperity gospel comes from a reading of the Old Testament where it is clear, particularly in parts of the Pentateuch (e.g. Deuteronomy 28), that success in battle, abundant harvests, and financial plenty were markers of divine favour.

If the origin for the emergence of this teaching within Pentecostalism must be found, it probably lies in the hearts and minds of the American Pentecostal preachers who lived through the dustbowl years of depression in the 1930s. Many of these grew up in grinding poverty with little education and a long way from any fulfilment of the American dream. The verse 'Beloved, I wish

above all things that thou mayest prosper and be in health, even as
thy soul prospereth' (3 John 2, AV) is said to have made a great
impact upon Yonggi Cho, the Korean pastor in Seoul. What these
preachers saw, and what they believed, was that poverty is a curse,
and they understood poverty after having known it at first hand.
These were not armchair Christians who had always had money to
spare. Rather, they were men and women who had gone hungry
and, for some of them, the condition of Christ on the cross was of
a man in the ultimate grip of poverty, without clothes, dignity,
food, or money. 'For you know the grace of our Lord Jesus Christ,
that though he was rich, yet for your sakes he became poor, so that
you through his poverty might become rich' (2 Corinthians 8.9)
was their understanding. More than this, Oral Roberts
(1918–2009), the leading American televangelist of the 1950s and
1960s, fastened on the words of Jesus in John 10.10: 'The thief
cometh not, but for to steal, and to kill, and to destroy: I am come
that they might have life, and that they might have it more
abundantly.' Christianity brought good things to those who
believed and was not to be understood as a message of perpetual
self-denial, self-abasement, or doubt.

If the preaching of the early prosperity gospellers was in reaction
to their own constricted upbringings, it is also clear that by the
1980s prosperity preaching had moved to a new level. It had
become more than an antidote to poverty. Rather, it had become a
central preoccupation of some American, and later African, Asian,
and Latin American, preachers. It had become the core of their
Christian message, and it was upheld most frequently by
extravagant television programmes which gobbled up money in
production costs. As a result, the televangelists found themselves
on a perpetual treadmill, having to appeal to their audience for
money in order to continue to preach, only in order that they
might appeal again for money, and so on. The early prosperity
gospel preachers came to understand that their appeals for money
must also be supported by benefits to their donors. They found the
words of Jesus, 'give and it shall be given on to you...' (Luke 6.38),

11. Oral Roberts, the American healing evangelist who began with tent crusades, moved successfully to radio and television, and ended by founding a university. He spanned the mid-20th century with an inventive ministry that bridged the divide between Pentecostals and charismatics

and they turned it into a doctrine or a spiritual law. They would encourage donations and then tell their hearers that, if they did this and if they imagined that their gifts were seeds, a wonderful harvest of plenty would follow.

Although Pentecostal academics, and many others, found the
behaviour of the healing evangelists thoroughly objectionable
and even deceitful, it is also true that a habit of generosity was
beneficial. It created a sort of trust not dissimilar from that
theorized by Pierre Bourdieu as 'social capital', and it enlarged
the horizons of men and women who had been at the bottom of
the economic scale and whose aspirations had almost been
snuffed out. During the 1950s and 1960s, when the Western
economy grew steadily, prosperity teaching circulated through
neo-Pentecostal and charismatic groups like the Full Gospel
Businessmen International. During the 1980s, it became
prevalent in West Africa, particularly Ghana and Nigeria, where
preachers tried to use the doctrine to lift the economic standards
of their populations. There seemed an almost magical
expectation that, by giving to pastors and supporting television
programmes, gross domestic product would soar. Among the
preachers to criticize this position was Mensa Otabil, the
independent-minded Ghanaian preacher, who appreciated that
economic advance depended upon commerce, education, and
trade and that these were the necessary tools for economic
self-improvement.

Some of the Pentecostal preachers formalized their teaching and
added to it a 'Word of Faith' dimension. The notion here was that
the words that people say determine the outcome of their lives.
Words become powerful tools or weapons by which lives are
directed and situations changed. Genesis speaks of the creation of
light by the very command of God, and other passages in the
Hebrew prophets indicate the determinative impact of God's
declarations whether of judgement or blessing. Protagonists
turned this phenomenon into 'positive confession' by which
declarations were made by preachers or individuals in the teeth of
adversity or desolation. The Christian who made a positive
declaration of this kind then only had to wait until their words
were fulfilled.

A few preachers went so far as to say that the words of believers in their mouths were as potent as the words of God in his mouth. Such a teaching appeared blasphemous, and yet it was based upon a perception of the world as governed by spiritual laws of cause and effect that were made by God and could not be broken. If, in a further development of this belief, God had given to Adam legal governance of the whole world, then those who were redeemed might re-obtain the authority that was lost by Adam's sin. Of course, such belief depended upon a literal interpretation of Genesis and, to the minds of many Pentecostals, an idiosyncratic one at that. Even so, the Word of Faith movement gained followers in parts of the Pentecostal world, particularly as the technique could be applied to quests for healing as well as to quests for prosperity. Make your declaration, agree with other believers that what you have declared will be so, and then wait in faith for its fulfilment. Such declarations, though they might be seen as a form of prayer, were always in danger of depersonalizing God and creating an obnoxious form of spiritual arrogance.

Smith Wigglesworth (1859–1947)

Wigglesworth was a gruff, uncompromising Yorkshire plumber from a poor English family. He was sent out to work in childhood and was unable to read and write until adult life. After conversion in a Wesleyan Methodist chapel, he married Polly, a Salvation Army officer. The two of them raised five children while Wigglesworth conducted his prospering plumbing business until, attending the 1907 Sunderland Conventions arranged by the Rev. Alexander Boddy, he received prayer from Mrs Boddy:

She laid hands on me in the presence of a brother. The fire fell and burned in me till the Holy Spirit clearly revealed absolute purity before God. At this point, she was called out of the room and during her absence a marvellous revelation took place, my body became full of light and Holy Presence, and in the revelation I saw an empty cross and at the same time the Jesus I loved and adored crowned in the Glory in a Reigning Position...I found to my glorious astonishment I was speaking in other tongues.

With a new confidence and boldness, he held public meetings in the United States, India, South Africa (where he prophesied to David du Plessis), Australia and New Zealand, Switzerland, Scandinavia, France, and Britain, and, according to eyewitness reports, saw astonishing healings. His bold faith and child-like confidence in the promises of Scripture made him an archetypal early Pentecostal: uneducated, unpredictable, unconventional, at home with the miraculous, and effective as an evangelist. Despite his lack of education, his sermons, which were recorded by short-hand and later published, contain vivid spiritual insights. He became a legend in his lifetime and is still seen as 'the apostle of faith' since faith, as the answer to every problem, was the constant theme of his preaching.

Exorcism

Pentecostals, from the beginning, believed in exorcism. Exotic stories told by missionaries returning from faraway places might include reference to exorcism but, until the charismatic movement in the 1960s began, it was unusual to hear any reference to exorcism taking place within the industrialized world. Once charismatic preachers began to challenge the settled opinions of early Pentecostals, dispute arose about the need for exorcism in the West. The debate became particularly acute when a small number of influential charismatic preachers argued that the exorcism ought, in some circumstances, to be performed on existing Christians. The debate polarized between those who argued that Christians who had accepted Christ and even known their own baptism in the Holy Spirit were, by this fact, clear of any

12. Smith Wigglesworth was a plumber from Bradford, England, who became the prototypical Pentecostal evangelist

demonic interference and, on the other side, those who argued
that all kinds of addictions and habits might have demonic origins
and, worse, that curses or occult behaviour practised by family
members might be passed down through the generations to today.
While the great majority of Pentecostals stood firm in their belief
in the completeness of their salvation, a minority of specialist
ministers propagated their own views about the prevalence of
demonic activity and the danger posed to unthinking Western
society of ignoring the threat of dark spiritual forces.

Spiritual warfare

The debate about exorcism was also partly a debate about
worldviews. By definition, the Pentecostal worldview included
reference to the Holy Spirit and, in this way, it opened up a whole
realm of unseen spiritual beings, whether angelic or demonic.
Pentecostals inevitably brought these beings into their
understanding of the modern and postmodern world. Such a
conjunction might appear unstable or ridiculous on the grounds
that invisible spiritual forces have no place in a world governed by
the soaring achievements of physics and the astonishing
revelations of contemporary genetics. Yet, as many surveys of
popular opinion have shown, most people in the West combine
admiration for science with quite unscientific beliefs and
practices. The industrial world is permeated by an acceptance of
astrology, fortune-telling, reincarnation, and dubious therapies.
Pentecostals, like many others, managed to integrate their belief
in the Holy Spirit and the supernatural realm with all the benefits
of a science-based civilization.

Even so, the emergence in the late 1980s of a 'spiritual warfare'
movement, while it claimed the allegiance of influential
charismatic leaders, stretched the credulity of many church
members and Pentecostal academics. For the most part, spiritual
warfare was taught by a group of preachers (including C. Peter
Wagner, C. H. Kraft, and G. Otis) whose influence greatly
exceeded their numbers. The movement recognized at the outset

that worldviews differed. Many of those who taught about spiritual warfare had travelled widely and noticed the thriving intense congregations in Latin America or Africa or Asia and the relative lukewarmness in Europe and North America. They attributed these differences to the post-Enlightenment worldview that prevailed in the industrialized world and the less mechanized and more spiritual worldview that prevailed elsewhere. At first, it appeared that the post-Enlightenment worldview needed to be challenged by miracles but, subsequently, it was argued that the real cause lay elsewhere.

At the end of one of Paul's epistles, Ephesians 6.12, the writer argues that 'our struggle is not against flesh and blood, but against the rulers, against the authorities, against the powers of this dark world and against the spiritual forces of evil in the heavenly realms'. Moreover, there is clearly exorcism in the Gospels of Matthew, Mark, and Luke (though not John) as well as in Acts. In the prophetic book of Daniel, there is a reference to Michael the Archangel who is thwarted by the 'Prince of the Persian kingdom' (Daniel 10.13f). When all these texts were assembled, a worldview was constructed in which powerful angelic beings were in charge of particular areas of the world and subordinate to these beings were individual demons. This was the kingdom of darkness organized in a strictly ranked fashion, and it was argued that these powerful angelic beings – seen as 'fallen angels' – were responsible for the spiritual darkness that prevailed in their territory. Indeed, these angelic beings were often called 'territorial spirits' and they were blamed for binding and blinding nations or populations against the gospel. A popular account of this worldview runs through the novels of Frank Peretti, whose *Piercing the Darkness* (1989) dramatizes the conflict.

What was strange to Christians sceptical of this analysis was that there is a clear teaching within the New Testament that Christians should submit to 'the powers that be' (Romans 13.1), that is, that they should not seek to overthrow the state but work within it. In the words of Christ, 'to render to Caesar the things which are Caesar's' (Matthew 22.21). It is difficult to understand why Christians should be law-abiding if the power of wicked spiritual beings lies behind legitimate earthly institutions. Nor is it clear how Christians should interpret texts which speak of the triumph of Christ over the forces of darkness (Colossians 2.15). In addition, academic Pentecostals pointed out that the mission of the church over 20 centuries had moved across the world at an astonishing rate without any recourse to the particular kinds of prayer that spiritual warfare demanded. Nevertheless, proponents of the view continued to argue that their explanation for the success of the gospel in some places and its relative failure in others could be attributed to the presence or absence of spiritual warfare.

In a later and softer development of the same kind of thinking, spiritual warfare was associated with a more holistic view of mission in which it was argued that the church should seek to influence an entire society and make changes to every aspect of it. There was a desire to transform rundown areas full of prostitution and drugs and to eliminate crime and make no-go urban areas once more suitable for law-abiding citizens. In rural areas, there was a desire to increase harvests and make subsistence farmers profitable and prosperous by tapping into new crops or farming methods or water reserves. In this way, some spiritual warfare preachers found a modified version of their doctrine gave them a fresh impetus and a fresh vision for a renewed society.

Conclusion

Though Pentecostals are known for the apparently impractical phenomenon of speaking in tongues, their faith is more often than not engaged with the ordinary struggles of life – with health, money, and how to live and to understand what is going on in the world.

Chapter 5

Churches and beliefs about the end of time

The early Pentecostals had a sense that time was being fulfilled, that they were being carried forward to an appointed destiny. Time was speeding along divinely controlled lines which stretched from the creation of the world to the return of Christ. Beyond this general sense that one day human history would come to an end, to an *eschaton*, a variety of schemes and interpretations ran through the early literature of Pentecostalism. Many of these were dispensational in that they were organized around a series of covenants whereby God dispensed grace to notable individuals – Adam, Abraham, Noah, Moses, and so on – and which were seen as the basis for God's dealing with the human race in a series of phases. Each phase ended in divine judgement, and all these phases were predetermined so that human choices could do little to change the sequence of events. Prophecy was 'history written in advance' by the Holy Spirit and could be, and was, simplified and drawn in long and complicated wall charts.

Other schemes were less deterministic and more inclined to place responsibility for the outcome of historical crises in the hands of the church. Consequently, the church was privileged to play a leading role in the epic drama of salvation and, though key events might be foreordained, there was plenty of scope for faith and heroism as the scroll of time unrolled.

Eschatology

It is difficult to describe the exact beliefs about the future held by the earliest Pentecostals. While there were dispensationalists who relied upon abstruse mathematical calculations based upon prophetic books in the Bible, others entertained generalized beliefs centred on the outpouring of the Holy Spirit. The crucial point was that the restoration of spiritual gifts to the church was seen as a sign of the 'last days'. Here, in the experience of speaking with other tongues, was an indication that the church, and therefore the world as a whole, was entering a new era. Charles Fox Parham, along with a small number of others, believed that speaking with tongues would enable rapid and powerful missionary work to occur, since the languages of the tongues-speakers were an indication of the countries to which they should go. And there were Pentecostal missionaries who went out thinking that they could speak Mandarin Chinese and who, on arrival in China, were dismayed to discover that they were mistaken. In hindsight, all this looks foolish, but what it shows is that the fervent expectation of these early Pentecostals was so intense that they were willing to travel across the world on the basis of an untested theological belief. Not all Pentecostals thought the tongues were given for missionary preaching – technically known as 'xenolalia' – and, in any case, the theory was soon proved to be wrong. What survived was an attitude to time and history which attributed prophetic significance to contemporary news.

Israel's role in the Bible and Zionism's role at the start of the 20th century were given a special importance, though, again, it is important to point out that only a minority of Pentecostals paid a great deal of attention to these matters. Those who did saw the people of Israel as having their own place within the final days of history. Some believed that there was a plan of salvation for the church and another plan for Israel and these two would move together in parallel. Others thought that the church had replaced

The Covenants

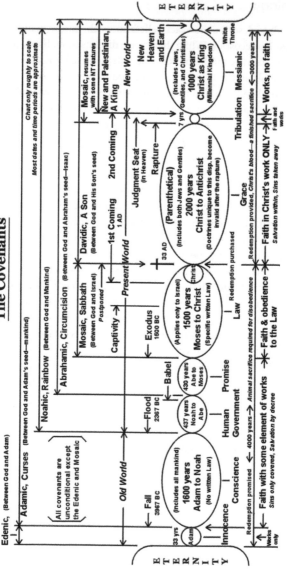

The Dispensations

13. A typical eschatological chart. There are several variations, but the one shown here gives a general sense of future foreordained events

Israel in the purposes of God and that the conversion of the Jews to Christianity was eventually going to occur. In any case, when the British government indicated its willingness for the Jewish people to return to Palestine in the 1920s, Pentecostals were among those who would have supported this move on the grounds that the establishment of a state of Israel was divinely intended. Although the Balfour Declaration was careful to insist upon the right of Arab peoples living in Palestine, the weight of support within the Pentecostal community would have been pro-Jewish. This position remained intact throughout the 20th century and was widely held among other kinds of conservative Christians, especially within the United States. Among the students of prophecy, there was an identification of Russia with Gog and Magog which moved south to attack Israel ('Son of man, set your face against Gog, of the land of Magog...prophesy against him...In future years you will invade a land that has recovered from war, whose people were gathered from many nations to the mountains of Israel...', Ezekiel 38.2, 8). Both in the 1930s when the Soviets made a pact with Hitler's anti-Semitic Germany and later, during the Cold War, support for Israel went hand in hand with opposition to Communist Russia.

While the 20th century took its course, early Pentecostal thinking about the future tended to be fixed upon the twin foci of the 'tribulation' and the 'rapture'. The tribulation was a period of intense religious persecution marked by earthquakes and culminating in the Antichrist's iron control of the global economic order. Before this devastating scenario unfolded, Pentecostals believed that the rapture would occur and that they would be snatched from the earth by the first return of Christ. These events have been popularized by the *Left Behind* series, whose books have sold millions of copies worldwide, and, before these, by Hal Lindsey's *The Late, Great Planet Earth*, published in 1970. Such expectations of the future were by no means confined to Pentecostals (the early preaching of Billy Graham included a pre-tribulation rapture), but they gave an urgency to Pentecostal evangelism since, by coming to faith before the tribulation occurred, one was guaranteed to escape it.

At various points in the 20th century, the tribulation appeared to be starting: the Great War (1914–18), the Jewish Holocaust (1939–45), the spectre of nuclear annihilation in the 1950s, and the Cuban Missile Crisis of 1962. If one wanted the graphic details of these events presented in a coded form, the Revelation of St John supplied them. Here, in a series of symbolic episodes, was everything from a vision of heaven to destruction, famine, plague, and hungry monsters attended by false prophets. By adopting a futurist interpretation of Revelation (i.e. an interpretation that presumed the events described there were in the future rather than had already occurred), a rich source of canonical information could be mined.

Such was the excited faith of the early Pentecostals that many of them did not expect to die. They thought that the rapture would occur in their own lifetimes. As the years passed, expectations changed. Damian Thompson's 2005 survey of the beliefs of Pentecostals at Kensington Temple (now London City Church) showed that, while a few members of the congregation engaged in a detailed prophetic study, most did not and that, though they believed Jesus would return, most thought that this would not take place in their own lifetimes. Their concerns were usually concentrated upon health and prosperity rather than tribulation and rapture. The gradual replacement of a theology revolving around tribulation and rapture was facilitated by a focus upon the kingdom of God. The idea of the kingdom of God could be stretched to include the ecumenical movement and secular society. To be orientated towards the kingdom was to accept the imperatives of social justice and the role that the church could play in the social arena. As Western Pentecostals became more middle class in the period after 1945, and as neo-Pentecostals came on the scene in the 1970s, a new mindset developed. It was not fearful of the tribulation but rather returned to an old Puritan view that foresaw the gradual dissemination of Christianity within an improving civilization. The only prophetic landmark on the horizon was the return of Christ, and this took place only after the gospel had been preached all over the earth (Matthew 24.14).

Consonant with this belief was an early Pentecostal position which had been popular and easy to understand and which did not require all the complex mental gymnastics of a dispensational interpretation of the Bible. Rather, there were only two relevant historical periods because the regular pattern of the rainfall in the holy land matched the pattern of the outpouring of the Holy Spirit in church history. There is an early fall of rain, the former rain, which falls at the time of planting and then, just prior to the harvest, the latter rain falls, and this fattens up the grain, olives, and grapes to make the crop fully ripe (Deuteronomy 11.14). The first outpouring of the Holy Spirit occurred after the Day of Pentecost when the church was planted. The latter rain, falling in the 20th century, is given for the sake of the harvest to ensure that the church grows abundantly prior to Christ's return. Here was an eschatological pattern everybody could appreciate and which made the outpouring of the Holy Spirit directly applicable to mission and evangelism.

Ecclesiology

Although Pentecostalism began in a revivalistic atmosphere at the beginning of the 20th century, and although there was great emphasis upon the work of the Holy Spirit within the life of the believer, Pentecostal congregations were mostly slow to develop all the implications of their theological ideas. Broadly speaking, Pentecostals who were fixated upon the end times thought in terms of a select Spirit-filled group who would escape the tribulation: they spoke of the 'bride of Christ', or even, using lesser-known parts of the Revelation of St John, of the 'manchild', and they cared little about the actual organization of the congregations. Their overriding classificatory category was one which existed within the mind of God and might never be made visible and embodied in any earthly organization. In other words, the church that will be raptured is not a denominational institution demarcated by sacraments but is made up of thousands of faithful individuals whose names are only known to God.

More practically orientated Pentecostals worked with a different scheme. Many of these had once been Methodists, or Baptists, or members of the Salvation Army, or Presbyterians, or one of any number of Protestant groups, and they came to their experience of the Spirit with basic assumptions about the necessity for human organization. True, some of them had crossed swords with denominational officials and this had left them with an antipathy to strong religious structures but, for many, the organizational machinery they had seen operating in Baptist or Methodist settings seemed perfectly acceptable.

Baptists are organized in a variety of ways, but the underlying principle of congregational autonomy is widespread. This is a system which gives power to individual congregations and which brings groups of congregations together by the method of ensuring that there is an agreed basis of belief. This basis of belief, or set of fundamental truths (or some such term), is the doctrinal foundation for cooperation and denominational union. The first step in setting up any denomination is therefore the hammering out of these fundamental beliefs so that congregations or ministers can accept them and join. Once these beliefs had been published, it was possible to see on a few sheets of paper what Pentecostals stood for. In the main, their beliefs were straightforwardly evangelical – they believed the Bible, the deity of Christ, the atonement, the return of Christ, and holy living – but they also accepted spiritual gifts as being restored to the church today. They endorsed water baptism by immersion as one of Christ's ordinances (rather than a sacrament) and believed that Holy Communion (or the Lord's Supper) is also commanded to all believers. In some respects, Pentecostals looked like 'evangelicals plus'. For nearly all of them, Communion was a simple memorial meal without any other theological overtones, although, in the case of Scandinavian Pentecostals, it might be asserted that the Communion service also conveyed physical healing. Whether this was universally or consistently believed is unclear and, in many instances, Pentecostals, even if they were Arminian in their theology (emphasizing the importance of free will), might well take the Calvinistic view of the Communion by believing that Christ was truly present through the work of the Spirit rather than by virtue of the bread and wine that are eaten and drunk.

If Pentecostal churches organized themselves on congregational principles, they might also borrow elements of Presbyterian forms of government. In this system, presbyteries (or groups of ministers elected to committees) would be given a diffuse and general power over the corporate activities of the denomination. Even if they had no explicit Presbyterian polity, as soon as Pentecostal congregations began to give money towards collective projects, this could be converted into the salaries of full-time officials who quickly took on some of the roles of overseers or superintendents. There was usually a balance between these officials and the sovereignty of the individual congregation, but, where Pentecostal churches had come out of episcopal Methodism, there was nothing to stop the creation of Pentecostal bishops with all the power over local clergy implicit in that system. Consequently, Pentecostal denominations could be divided into two broad types: those which protected congregational autonomy while encouraging participation in denominational activities through general assemblies where debates could occur and decisions be made by voting; and those which emphasized the importance of leadership vested in individuals who might or might not be called bishops and who had the power to appoint ministers to congregations whether these congregations liked it or not. A. J. Tomlinson of the Church of God was quite clear that 'Jesus instituted his church for government...his church means government', whereas in the kind of system found in the Assemblies of God, this sort of talk would never have been tolerated.

Pentecostal denominations tend, therefore, to differ in their systems of government rather than in their basic beliefs or core practices. Some of these systems of government might imply that church property would be owned by the denomination rather than by the individual congregation. As time passed, church properties increased in value, and there was always the possibility that a particular congregation which, over several years, had sacrificially given money to buy the building became depleted. Denominational officials, whether they were bishops or superintendents, might then move in to sell the building over the protesting heads of the remaining members of the congregation. In one Pentecostal denomination (the Elim Pentecostal Church in Britain), the congregations had first been established out of a series of highly successful healing campaigns led by George Jeffreys in the 1920s and 1930s. Originally, ownership of the buildings had been vested in the denomination but, late in the 1930s, Jeffreys began to argue that such a system was undemocratic and to contend that church members should be allowed to hold the trust deeds of their own buildings and dispose of them as they wished. As a result, the denomination now has several categories of property ownership, some held centrally and others locally.

The Scandinavian Pentecostals (influenced by Lewi Pethrus) disagreed strongly with the prevalent opinion elsewhere. Scandinavian Pentecostals believed that the local congregation was paramount. They positively rejected any organization beyond the local church or which in any way compromised the autonomy of the local church. For instance, missionary work in Scandinavia was organized congregationally. Missionaries were sent out from individual congregations rather than from the pooled resources of a group of congregations organized into denominations. More than this, Scandinavian Pentecostal churches refused to establish any printed doctrinal beliefs that might be used as a foundation for cooperation – this smacked to them of a 'human creed'. Their people would meet together for conferences but would never decide anything that had collective implications; ministerial gatherings would not become decision-making sessions. Rather, the local church, and the local church members' meeting, was elevated in importance. The Scandinavian model gave great power to the local pastor, particularly when this pastor presided over urban congregations with many thousands of members, and, despite pressure from Pentecostals in other parts of the world, the Scandinavians continued to work in the way that they believed to be right. When the first European Pentecostal Conference was arranged in 1939, there was no retreat from these principles and no supra-denominational structure came into being. The Scandinavian model was influential in Latin America, especially Brazil, and in parts of Africa and Asia where Scandinavian missionaries took their message and empowered their converts. Nevertheless, the Scandinavian model did allow vigorous urban congregations to bring smaller satellite congregations into existence on a mother/daughter principle, and cynics might argue that the mother churches and their pastors actually became leaders of what were effectively localized denominations.

Regardless of the way the government of Pentecostal churches was designed, the crucial and distinctive question about the life of Pentecostal congregations was addressed only in the 1920s and 1930s. What were the implications of believing that every single member of a Pentecostal congregation was filled by the Holy Spirit and therefore able to voice a prophecy or manifest some other charismatic gift? The British Pentecostal writer Donald Gee began to work out a participatory ecclesiology that showed how the various gifts of the Holy Spirit might contribute to an overall church meeting. The Holy Spirit democratized Pentecostalism by distributing spiritual gifts widely so that, if there was a secret to Pentecostal growth, it lay with this capacity of Pentecostal churches to energize every member. In a sacramental or liturgical church, the professional clergy read the services and lead the prayers while the congregation is restricted to prayerbook responses or other minor contributions. In the Pentecostal congregation, every Spirit-filled member might have vital light to shed on what should be done next because every member is in some sense a minister.

A harmoniously functioning Pentecostal congregation might begin to resemble the Pauline description of the church in Corinth:

> What then shall we say, brothers? When you come together, *everyone* has a hymn, or a word of instruction, a revelation, a tongue or an interpretation. All of these must be done for the strengthening of the church.
>
> (1 Corinthians 14.26, my italics)

Here was a congregation that valued the contribution of every member and, because it did so, every gathering was unpredictable. This gave a sense of excitement to attendees of Pentecostal congregations: they did not know what to expect next because the Spirit might move anyone to do anything. Visitors to Pentecostal congregations which function in this way are often surprised at the 'organized chaos' of the meetings. Actually, these meetings settle down into discernible patterns with many variants and, in this respect, resemble a jam session of jazz musicians where each instrumentalist provides an impromptu solo that adds up to a satisfying new composition. By contrast, the liturgical service resembles a classically orchestrated production following a written score in which there is no room for improvisation.

The freedom found in Pentecostal congregations is impressive, but it is a delicate freedom. If it moves too far in one direction, it is lost when dominant individuals begin to hold sway over other members of the congregation and, by inflating their own spiritual gifting, suppress everyone else's. If it moves too far in the direction of ministerial control, services will start to run with a clockwork precision that transforms Pentecostal congregations into energetic singing machines. The balance between freedom within the congregation and freedom within the ministerial cohort is difficult to achieve. What Pentecostal churches aim for is the presence of spiritual gifts within the congregation as well as the presence of spiritual gifts within the lives and work of their ministers. As Pentecostals strive to achieve this freedom, they do so by noting that the restoration of spiritual gifts also logically leads to a belief in the restoration of the role of apostles, prophets, pastors, and teachers. In short, Pentecostalism invokes a double restoration to the life of the church. This logic was quickly picked up at the beginning of the 20th century by the Apostolic Church in Wales, and later relaunched with great effect after 1948 in what came to be called the 'Latter Rain revival'.

In essence, the Latter Rain movement, which began in Canada and spread to other parts of North America and then more widely still through the itinerant healing evangelists, was premised upon the appearance of gifted new apostles, prophets, and evangelists. Within a short time, these new claimants ran into heavy opposition from denominational officials, Pentecostal bishops, and other members of Pentecostal organizations. The Latter Rain protagonists, being independent of denominational control, saw themselves as initiating a renewal movement within Pentecostalism designed to return the churches to the early free-flowing days of the Azusa Street revival and its immediate aftermath. About 40 years had passed from the beginnings of Pentecostalism, and here was a new downpour of the Spirit to bring the supernatural refreshment which over-organized and over-bureaucratized Pentecostal denominations had lost. Prophets would prophesy, eschatologically amazing miracles of revelation and healing would follow, religious organization would wither away, and the church would return to apostolic vibrancy. Such was the hope.

As the years passed, the Latter Rain movement fizzled out. Yet, it left a legacy that was to be fulfilled in an unexpected way. In the

1960s, the charismatic movement began. This was the arrival of Pentecostal or Pentecostal-style experiences within the traditional mainline denominations. All over the world in Lutheran, Episcopalian, Methodist, Baptist, Brethren, Roman Catholic, Anglican, and other churches, men and women began to speak with other tongues, to pray for healing, and sing the songs that Pentecostals had for so long enjoyed. The Pentecostals understood the Spirit to have been poured out upon the rest of the church. The movement was interdenominational and expressed its interdenominational nature in big international conferences where denominational differences were eclipsed by a common mode of worship and shared spiritual experiences.

The charismatic movement inevitably asked ecclesiological questions of the Pentecostals. For instance, while Pentecostals had believed that the experience of the Holy Spirit followed evangelical conversion ('new birth'), Roman Catholics who experienced glossolalia fitted their explanation of this experience into a sacramental theology of initiation which believed in the impartation of the Spirit at infant baptism. Similarly, while Pentecostals were, in many cases, open to the notion of 20th- and 21st-century apostles and prophets, many of the mainline denominations found these ideas impossible to stomach – and they would have been very difficult to fit within the traditional hierarchies of Roman Catholicism or Anglicanism. Even so, the charismatic movement brought Pentecostals into contact with mainline denominations, and official dialogues began to take place between Pentecostals and Roman Catholics and between Pentecostals and the Reformed church. However, these prolonged theological discussions were of little interest to emerging radical charismatics who began to break free of the charismatic movement but did not want to join the Pentecostals either. They did not want the administrative machinery that many Pentecostal denominations had accumulated. Nor did they want to remain within mainline denominations which, despite welcoming the Spirit, left intact too many historic structures and precedents.

David du Plessis (1905–87)

The Afrikaans-speaking David du Plessis was born in South Africa, converted and baptized by the Apostolic Faith Mission (AFM), but rose quickly through denominational ranks and eventually served as editor of its bilingual magazine, *Comforter/Trooster*, and became a reforming administrator. After receiving a remarkable prophecy in 1936 from Smith Wigglesworth about his future role, du Plessis attended the first Pentecostal World Conference in Zurich in 1947 and, resigning from the AFM, served as the conference's organizing secretary for many years. His charm, humour, and down-to-earth preaching were coupled with the improbable (but correct) belief that Pentecostalism would eventually spread across to the mainline denominations. Breaking out of the narrowness of his religious upbringing, he began to move in ecumenical circles, where he was known as 'Mr Pentecost'. He was involved in the World Council of Churches and helped foster understanding between Pentecostals and the Roman Catholic Church after Vatican II; he is seen as one of those rare individuals who shaped 20th-century Christianity.

From the 1970s, these radical charismatics started what were first called 'house churches' and later 'new churches' or apostolic networks. These networks were characterized by two distinct features. First, as the name implies, they believed in modern-day apostles who had the ability to plant churches and lead spiritual advance. Apostles were men (usually) who were spiritually gifted and who had a proven capacity to initiate and run churches. They were people who gradually gathered churches around them, sometimes by attracting small independent congregations in need of a mentor, and at other times by building their own large congregations which they subsequently used as a base of operations for a travelling ministry. Second, the churches were deliberately organized on relational lines – by which they meant that these congregations were not to be governed by constitutions, committees, church meetings, voting, or other purportedly non-biblical decision-making methods found in most denominations. Rather, the churches were to be led by apostles who would be guided by charismatic gifts of revelation and knowledge and loosely networked to each other by being connected with the apostle. The apostle was a kind of bishop, although different from other kinds because the role was not defined by a written constitution. In the best apostolic networks, the stress on relationships and the lack of a constitution led to a refreshing emphasis upon the grace of God.

Conclusion

The earliest Pentecostals believed they were a short distance away from the dramatic events that would herald the return of Christ. They could interpret international events against a dark prophetic scheme though, as the years passed, interpretations adjusted and brightened. Congregations were built and gradually developed the distinctive character of widespread lay involvement implied by Spirit-baptism.

Chapter 6
Megachurches, cells, and progressive Pentecostalism

There have always been famously large congregations, and many of these have not been Pentecostal. The phenomenon of the megachurch takes size a stage further. The megachurch is qualitatively different from a large congregation because the sheer accumulation of resources and personnel enables all kinds of non-conventional activities to be supported. For instance, the neo-Pentecostal City Harvest in Singapore, with a membership of over 24,000, employs over 150 full-time staff engaged in a mixture of administrative and specialist concerns. There are staff to deal with the elderly, the mentally handicapped, music activities, education, many language groups, and electronic media. Because all megachurches expect their members to give money towards the funding of the entire operation, large sums of disposable income can be deployed. Whereas in the Middle Ages Christian congregations would express their piety in soaring, intricately decorated stone cathedrals taking several generations to build, the modern megachurch makes do with indoor arenas or purpose-built complexes that rarely invest in aesthetic architecture. The emphasis is on doing and communicating.

The Pentecostal or charismatic megachurch has begun to appear all over the world, particularly in Asia and Latin America, but also in North America and to a lesser extent in Europe.

Megachurches and cells

Early on a Sunday morning on the island of Yoido in the city of Seoul, Korea, uniformed marshals appear ready to direct the traffic. Soon afterwards, street vendors begin to set up their stalls ready to offer snacks to the arriving crowds. Then printed notices and bundles appear in preparation for the collection of discarded clothes and recyclable materials. The first of seven services of the day begins at 7 am and runs absolutely punctually because, if it is delayed, the timing of the rest of the day is affected. Crowds begin to stream in for the next service. Coaches arrive. The pavement is thronged and the crowd waits in a cordoned-off area at the bottom of the main steps leading to the auditorium. When the previous service ends, the first crowd of 12,000 streams out and the new crowd streams in, some of the people running to secure their favourite seats.

Inside, the auditorium is built like a vast theatre with ground-level seats and then upper tiers facing towards the platform where the ministers, in restrained ecclesiastical robes, will sit or kneel to pray. Above their heads are a large bare wooden cross and screens displaying notices for the coming week or fast-moving MTV-style video clips fastening on to an aspect of the church's ministry. Visitors are ushered to seating areas upstairs where they can put on headphones and receive simultaneous translation of the service in one of half a dozen languages.

A full-robed choir is seated beside the platform facing the congregation and an orchestra, complete with a conductor, are also ready for the start. When the service begins, perhaps with a trumpet fanfare, the music rises to a crescendo, the choir sings recognizably Western tunes, the screens provide the words of songs in Korean, and the entire process, a little like a smooth theatrical production, unfurls with silken precision. If the congregation is asked to pray, people respond with noisy enthusiasm and all pray aloud at once until the moment passes.

14. David Yonggi Cho: the founder pastor of Yoido Full Gospel Church

The sermon is biblical, carefully structured, and simple to understand. When the service ends, there is a brief pause at the changeover. Visitors, if they wish, can then take a free coach journey to a mountain reserved for prayer and fasting. If there is an overflow crowd at the midday gathering, screens on the outside of the building relay what is going on inside for those who sit on the pavement area. It is difficult to work out exactly how many people attend the Sunday meetings, but up to 100,000 people are probably involved.

Yoido Full Gospel Church is a megachurch. Starting with five people in 1958, it has grown to well over half a million. This raises the questions of how this has happened and what kind of church emerges once such large numbers are assembled under a single leader. The growth of Yoido occurred in three phases, the first in the immediate aftermath of the Korean War that resulted in the division of the nation. David Yonggi Cho began preaching a message of healing and material uplift until, in 1961 a Full Gospel Revival Centre was constructed. By 1964, with its name changed to Full Gospel Central Church, the membership reached 3,000. Working continuously, Cho suffered a breakdown in health that put him in hospital. While reading Exodus 18, he received a revelation. Just as Moses had reorganized Israel, he would reorganize his congregation into a collection of cell-units, each under their own local leader. He would retain the big Sunday preaching time but, on week nights, he would utilize homes where small groups could gather for prayer and Bible study. In the second phase, he asked his male deacons to take over this role, but they refused to do so. Here Cho showed his countercultural edge. Korean society, with a strong Confucian background, had minimized the leadership potential of women. Cho appointed the women as deacons and then asked them to take charge of their home groups. The women proved to be highly effective. Little groups were started all over Seoul in tower blocks and apartments. Each cell-unit followed a pattern of hospitality, prayer, Bible study, and concern for the local poor. In the third phase, the present new building was constructed (1973), a prayer mountain was purchased (1973), a publishing company opened (1976), and a weekly newspaper was started (1978). The church grew dramatically, and by 1979 had reached 100,000 people. In 1993, its educational facility became the International Theological Institute.

The megachurch must be highly organized. Cho divided metropolitan Seoul into 13 districts and a senior pastor is assigned over each district. The districts were then subdivided and given sub-pastors, of which, by 2005, there were 309. And then the subdistricts are divided into sections, of which there were 4,374, and, within these, the cell-units are located, and there were 11,214 of these. The system allows enormous resources to be mobilized and personal care to be expressed despite the inherent dangers of anonymity within such a large enterprise.

In Cho's case, it was theological insight that led to the setting up of cell-units in his church. The theology of cell church has been subsequently developed by arguing either that all living organisms are made up of cells (and therefore the church as a body of people must follow the same principle) or that the early church began in the home. Paul writes, 'greet Priscilla and Aquila, my fellow workers... greet also the church that meets in their house' (Romans 16.1,5), indicating that New Testament Christians all over the Gentile world met in the houses of their members – indeed, there were no specialist church buildings until around the year 200 CE. This resulted in several types of gathering. The cell is the smallest and most intimate; beyond this is the congregation made up of numerous cell groups; beyond this again is the grand celebration or convocation that is made up of lots of congregations. The balance between the differently sized groups is one aspect of the 'chopstick theology' of Cho. One chopstick can pick up nothing, but two working opposite each other can deal with any food.

15. The Yoido Full Gospel Church. This is reputed to be the largest congregation in the world

Whatever the theological basis for cell churches, the sociological grounds are also substantial. The 20th century saw rapid urbanization as, in every part of the globe, farm workers migrated to conurbations looking for work. Within these conurbations, transport links, often utilizing underground electric trains, have shuttled a commuting public in and out of offices and shopping malls. The same trains move church members around their cities. Where 19th-century New York led the way, others followed. Skyscrapers and office or apartment blocks crowded the skyline all over the new cities of the world: within zones of great population density, cell groups are an ideal social structure. They can transform the tone of the neighbourhood by random acts of kindness, create a family feeling, and remove insignificance from those who feel lost in the faceless urban crowd. In sociological terms, they confront the depersonalization brought about by the pervasiveness of technology; where human–machine interactions outnumber human–human interactions, cells protect against the encroachments of alienation.

Beyond all this, the megachurch becomes a visible expression of Christianity. From the inside, it provides a support system to its members and a way of addressing contemporary problems. Members of the church can and do collect money for charitable projects which, as individuals, they could make little impact upon. Yoido has provided money for heart surgery for many hundreds of people and sent food supplies all over the world. It has a village for the elderly and exemplary ecological projects. Outside the megachurch, its values can begin to impact upon a city or a nation. Most megachurches include broadcasting studios and, as fibreoptic cables become faster and bandwidth wider, video-streaming becomes ever more capable of converging with other forms of television. The interaction between religious values and social or economic values lies behind Max Weber's thesis that capitalism and Protestantism were connected in the trajectory of European history. The visitor to Yoido, seeing its efficient organization and motivational video presentations, notices that some of its leading members work in the world-class Korean electronics industry: what succeeds in church may succeed in commerce, and vice versa.

Yet, despite their success, cell-based churches have not avoided criticism. Both theologically and sociologically, there are several rationales for the cell principle. At its simplest, and in the style advocated by Cho, the cell-unit is a small meeting for prayer, Bible study, and evangelism in the home. In other types of cell, the discipleship role is underlined and the number of cell meetings per week is increased to cope with the training of cell group leaders. In some variations of the cell philosophy, the dangers of excessive control appear to have been realized, especially when the cells are arranged in a hierarchy. European and North American churches, situated in democratic cultures that thrive on individual freedom of expression, recoil from what appears cultish. In these countries, and where congregations draw upon a rural hinterland, it is the main church building that serves as the usual venue for the megachurch's numerous activities. In these situations, there is little devolution of pastoral ministry to the leaders of small groups, and cells hardly feature.

Megachurches and leadership

Megachurches are almost always associated with an individual leader who has built them up. The problem of handing over leadership when the recognized superstar dies or retires can be solved by letting the leader-designate serve alongside the old leader for a period of transition. Beneath the top level of leadership, there are numerous others in charge of geographical areas or subsidiary ministries.

One of the secrets of Pentecostal life and growth lies in the enormous range of opportunities given to men and women of many different talents to express their faith. When they are most rapidly growing, Pentecostal churches require many administrators, preachers, teachers, care workers, worship leaders, and others. The life of the church is geared around growth. At the same time, the need for people to take responsibility for facets of the enterprise also requires in-house training and staff development courses. People who are short of self-confidence will take numerous small steps in the setting of the church that will later enable them to become confident in the secular workplace. Conversely, those with expertise in the secular workplace will find an opportunity to apply their skills within the context of the church. Willingness to engage in training together with belief in the empowerment of the Holy Spirit make a potent combination. Cho's training of his female deacons as home group leaders is one example of many that could be given. Moreover, in many places, no distinction is made between the ministry of men and women, so that, in traditionally male-dominated cultures, the church offers an arena where women are educated and can develop their non-domestic skills.

Megachurches, denominations, and networks

Megachurches have an ambiguous relationship with denominations. On the one hand, megachurches are so large and self-contained that their senior pastors enjoy a status similar to that of denominational leaders. The megachurch can survive without denominational support and may, indeed, find denominational by-laws irksome. The temptation to the megachurch pastor is to break free of what are perceived to be denominational shackles, especially where denominational funds are supported by payments calculated as a fixed proportion of congregational income. The megachurch may well feel that it does not want to pay substantial sums of money to support the activities of denominational officials whose *raison d'être* might be thought of as the enforcement of regulation and the creation of yet more regulation. In short, the denomination needs the megachurch far more than the megachurch needs the denomination. In any event, megachurch leaders may find they have more in common with other megachurch leaders – even if these megachurches come from different doctrinal streams within Pentecostalism – than with their own denominational officials with whom they should theoretically see eye to eye. On the other hand, megachurches often began in a denominational setting and may have borrowed money from denominational accounts or simply be loyal to their heritage. Even the megachurch may think twice before severing its denominational bonds.

The result of this imbalance of power is that megachurch pastors may also become denominational leaders. This is particularly the case where denominational leaders are elected because of obvious success. Who better to lead your denomination than someone who has managed to build a large and thriving congregation? Yet this still leaves the question of how the megachurch should relate to its own denomination. Where megachurch pastors are also denominational leaders, they may decide to create a network within a denomination and use the language of the radical apostolic groups to explain or justify the process. This looks contradictory because the networks have argued that they are *not* denominations and want to avoid bureaucracy like the plague. Yet the megachurch has so many resources at its disposal that it can pay for numerous activities. If these activities are supportive of denominational life, the megachurch pastor will be appreciated and the tensions between the big barons of the megachurch and the common pastors of the denomination will dissipate.

A different kind of relationship occurs where the megachurch is neo-Pentecostal, that is, it does not belong to a denomination. Here, the megachurch often becomes a flagship congregation, able to fund the activities of the apostolic figure who is constantly travelling from city to city and from country to country meeting with local leaders, speaking at large conferences, and bringing wisdom to bear upon countless local circumstances. In this model, the megachurch is the home of the apostle in a collaborative network of congregations that make every effort to avoid the ethos and paraphernalia of denominationalism. Here, the megachurch serves as the evidence that the apostolic figure is what he (or she) claims to be. The megachurch is not in these circumstances a problem for the denomination to solve but an expression of apostolicity.

Megachurches and the cultural mandate

Megachurches are conscious of their relationship with culture. Their sheer size and vibrancy enables them to create a microclimate for Christians. Some megachurches, particularly those in the United States, offer little-league baseball, basketball, holidays, schooling, help with home schooling, a special pastor to visit those in need of coronary care, mission trips, local radio broadcasts, a restaurant, a bookshop, a refuge for single mothers, a counselling centre for women considering abortion, musical productions, and so many agencies that they could be thought of as akin to a shopping mall. Everything you need is to be found within the megachurch and, in it, your faith is sheltered from erosion.

The 'shopping mall' image for the megachurch only applies in some instances. Others, rather than seeking to provide a protected total environment for members, wish to engage secular culture. This notion may be undergirded by a theology of mission or by a theology of common grace built upon the belief that all human beings are made in the image of God and that therefore all culture, as a human production, ought to reflect the divine image. Either way, the so-called 'cultural mandate' will validate Christians who feel called to serve to the marketplace, politics, or the media. Early holiness teaching would have taught the precise opposite: Christians should shun the world, its fashions and recreations. Early Pentecostal churches were noted for their strict avoidance of tobacco, alcohol, the cinema, and other marks of worldliness. By contrast, the newer Pentecostal churches believe they are tasked to go out into contemporary culture. As a result, their music interfaces with pop or rock culture to the extent that their worship services, with stroboscopic lights and high-quality audio and video equipment, resemble concerts. Equally, Pentecostal churches may set up businesses or, as we shall see, broadcasting outlets. Pentecostal preachers may become motivational speakers at business seminars and express their views on impending legislation in public debate. The mode and tone is ultra-modern and attractive to the young.

Progressive Pentecostalism

The worldwide extent of Pentecostalism means that it exists in numerous cultural and political contexts. In its apostolic form, it is engaged primarily in church planting. In its denominational form, so Miller and Yamamori estimate, about 15% of churches are engaged in programmatic social activity. In their definition of progressive Pentecostalism, they exclude social action that is instrumental or for the purpose of ensuring evangelical

16. Hillsongs Church: an example of a contemporary transformative Pentecostal church reaching out to young professionals in large international cities

17. Kaka: a world-famous Brazilian footballer with Pentecostal connections

conversion. The progressive Pentecostals they identify are involved in social action either out of theological conviction or because their congregations are made up of those who were once poor and remember their roots. Such progressive Pentecostals may be found in Guatemala, Brazil, India, sub-Saharan Africa, inner-city

America, and Asia. They tend not be connected with Pentecostal churches caught up in the health and wealth prosperity gospel. Nor are they especially identified with Pentecostal churches that have a political agenda, since their mode of operation tends to exclude NGOs or government programmes. These Pentecostal churches are more interested in growing their own leaders and setting up their own welfare organizations from the grassroots up. Their outreaches tend to be firmly planted *inside* the life of a congregation rather than being adjunct to freestanding organizations funded and run by others. Their impetus needs to be understood in the context of the congregational worship and the perceived experience of the Holy Spirit as the guide, or 'senior partner', in these initiatives.

The work of progressive Pentecostals may also be linked with the belief that it is the duty of the church to transform the world, and such a belief may be derived from a theology of the kingdom of God. Or, to put this another way, a belief in the kingdom of God is connected with the hope that the earth will be redeemed. This implies that farmland should be cultivated to yield more abundant crops and that the material environment, whether landscape or cityscape, may be miraculously transformed. After researching progressive Pentecostals in 20 different countries and conducting more than 300 interviews, Miller and Yamamori found the following:

> efforts to feed, clothe and shelter people; drug rehabilitation programs; HIV/AIDS interventions; micro-enterprise loans, especially to women; visitation of people in prison, as well as support systems for their families; attempts at family reunification, including divorce intervention and bridging programs between teenagers and their parents; pregnancy counselling; ministries to prostitutes and sex workers; medical and dental services; services to the elderly and handicapped; schools and educational assistance programs for children; residential programs for street children and orphans; efforts to counteract racial prejudice and other forms of discrimination.

They classify these programmes under eight headings:

Mercy ministries (e.g. food, clothing, shelter);

Emergency services (e.g. floods, famine, and earthquakes);

Education (e.g. day care, schools, tuition assistance);

Counselling services (e.g. addiction, divorce, depression);

Medical assistance (e.g. health clinics, dental clinics, psychological services);

Economic development (e.g. micro-enterprise, job training, affordable housing);

Appreciation of the arts (e.g. music, dance, drama);

Policy change (government corruption, community organizing).

Sociological reflection

The master narrative of the sociology of religion is the story of secularization. As modernity has advanced, the world has become disenchanted; as rationality and technology have filled up the spaces where mystery used to be, religion has been removed; as religion has been removed, its institutional presence and association with political power have been diminished. This story, supported by numerous falling statistical indices of religious rites of passage, has been favoured by European sociologists like Steve Bruce who have illustrated their account by reference to Christianity. But it is a story that could be told another way. While Christianity in Europe appears to be on the retreat in the face of rationality and modernity, Christianity in the United States, equally rational and equally modern, appears unaffected. An alternative account suggests that religiosity is simply being expressed in new ways, ways that no longer depend upon institutional forms. People 'believe without belonging', and their religiosity is expressed by the eclectic mixture of doctrines and practices in what has been called 'flexidoxy', or composite beliefs that are acceptable because they benefit the self. Such a diffuse style of faith may be fed by numerous suppliers of religion offering their wares to a consumerist population.

Sociological theories of religion have to take account of Pentecostalism and various proposals have been floated, some with empirical support and others without it, to explain what is going on. One suggestion is that Pentecostalism offers an experiential form of religion that is compatible with experiential cultural styles. Rationality, while it informs one dimension of society, does not drive the culture of the young. Here, expressive individualism is the order of the day. This type of individualism has roots in the 19th-century Romantic Movement and celebrates the primacy of emotion. According to Robert Bellah, another type of individualism, utilitarian individualism, is derived from an economic understanding of human existence. Here people stress freedom to pursue their goals through property and commerce. As a counterbalance to individualism of all types, the community should be strengthened. Communitarian ethics emphasize the common good which may, indeed, include the good of the individual. What we see in the megachurch – but actually in any large congregation – is the creation of a community of believers who may, in their musically enhanced worship, give play to their expressive impulses while, through the practical teaching they receive on how to live, harness their utilitarian concerns. The megachurch becomes a 'transformational community' able to provide an environment where altruism is practised on a large scale and where Christianity takes on transnational dimensions.

What seems clear is that the old distinctions between the church (co-terminus with national or even international boundaries), the denomination (accepting the validity of other expressions of faith), and the sect (claiming a unique and exclusive access to God and standing apart from society) are beginning to break down or be permutated. Megachurches can hardly be described as sects because they interface with every level of the societies in which they are situated and, though early Pentecostals may have been sect-like in their outlook, their more recent diversification has meant that it would be possible to find examples of each sociological category across the diverse domain of global

Pentecostalism with its thousands of groupings and numerous streams. David Martin has counterpointed Pentecostalism in Latin America with Catholicism and shown how Pentecostalism's portable, lay identity has given it an adaptability that is particularly appealing to the aspiring poor, young males, and women. An alternative and more limited hypothesis has argued that Pentecostalism functions best in cultures where its spiritual worldview is compatible with that of the indigenous culture: if the indigenous culture has room for spirits, Pentecostalism, with its belief in the potency of the Holy Spirit, makes a perfect fit. The trouble with this hypothesis is that it appears to be designed to explain what is happening in Africa or Latin America but unable to cope with North America or Westernized Asia. It is perhaps more believable that, despite cultural and national differences, human beings are remarkably similar all over the world and that, in the face of the perpetual existential challenges of family relationships, meaning, alienation, and death, explanations of Pentecostalism's success should be looked for in our commonalities.

Conclusion

Megachurches match the urbanization of the contemporary world and, within these complicated and creative structures, Christians can either live in a protected environment or else be prepared for engagement with contemporary culture. The older unworldly congregations of holiness are being transformed into high-tech communities of faith attractive to young people. From these and other bases, Pentecostals can launch humanitarian projects.

Chapter 7
Race, ecumenism, and politics

In her book on Christianity in this series, Linda Woodhead distinguishes between church and biblical Christianity, on the one hand, which locate the power of faith externally and which focus upon the Father and the Son, and, on the other hand, mystical Christianity, which locates the power of faith internally and which focuses upon the Holy Spirit. Pentecostal Christianity falls within the second category: it is the internal power of the Holy Spirit that is basic.

In his book on theology in this series, David Ford proposes a theological spectrum between, at one extreme, a theology that is shaped by 'some contemporary philosophy, worldview, or practical agenda' and, at the other extreme, a theology that attempts to 'repeat a scriptural worldview, classic theology, or traditional version of Christianity'. We may join together what Woodhead and Ford are saying by anticipating that different types of theology will create different institutional structures and forms. We could say that the theology of Christianity shapes its life and, in combination with its social or cultural context, determines its contemporary expression. In the Sermon on the Mount, Jesus said 'neither do men pour new wine into old wineskins. If they do, the skins will burst, the wine will run out and the wineskins will be ruined. No, they pour new wine into new wineskins, and both are preserved.' Pentecostals have seen the Holy Spirit as new wine, and the new wineskins as new organizational principles by which the life and power of the Spirit is held. For better or worse, race, politics, and broadcasting have historically shaped these organizational principles.

Race

In its early days and at its height, the Azusa Street revival was noted for its interracial freedom. Blacks and whites mingled with each other, prayed with each other, hugged each other, and took part in the same disorganized services. Because it was situated outside the South, Los Angeles was not subject to the United States' restrictive segregationist laws. And, in any case, Los Angeles was a burgeoning city at the end of the railroad. There were Hispanic, Mexican, European, and Chinese immigrants arriving almost daily, and some of these found their way to the Azusa Street meetings. Frank Bartleman, an eyewitness to these events, famously reported that the 'colour line is washed away in the blood [of Jesus]', by which he meant that all racial divisions were ignored in the fervour of revival.

Later, when North American Pentecostal denominations were established and developed, some of them became almost entirely white and others almost entirely black. A few managed to retain an interracial polity – the largest of these being the Church of God (Tennessee), although the Assemblies of God retained its Hispanic congregations by organizing them into a separate section. In South Africa, when Pentecostalism arrived with the preaching of John G. Lake, a man who had attended Azusa Street and been influenced by its message, the earliest congregations were mixed but, eventually, schism occurred. What tended to happen was that the leaders of emerging denominations were white and, when black ministers found themselves discriminated against or excluded from denominational office, they broke away to form their own groupings.

The record of Pentecostal denominations during the later apartheid era in South Africa is not an honourable one. The Apostolic Faith Mission (AFM), even from its earliest days, baptized whites and blacks separately, and this policy was then hardened when the National Party took power after 1948. In pandering to Afrikaner dominance, the AFM quietened down its meetings so as to sound more like the favoured Reformed churches and thereby gain permission to preach on state-controlled radio. At the same time, and in keeping with its nationalistic aspirations, the AFM dropped its pacifist stance. The vice-president of the AFM, G. R. Wessels, was made a National Party senator. Only after 1994 did the AFM turn around, confess apartheid as a sin, and unify with the black churches.

One interpretation of these events is that Pentecostalism in Azusa Street was a harbinger of racial harmony and an example of the theological reality that the Holy Spirit makes no distinctions between the usual categories by which the human race divides itself up. Ethnicity, gender, age, nationality, and class are all transcended by the inclusiveness of divine love. Only later, when the spiritual fire cooled, did normal social categories reassert themselves and Pentecostalism accommodated itself to injustice. In South Africa, early AFM leaders climbed onto the back of the racist tiger and later fell off and were devoured by it. They began by accepting segregation (without accepting hard-line racism) but ended with the doctrine of apartheid that legalized, institutionalized, and brutally enforced white control of majority black and coloured populations. There were AFM dissidents like Frank Chikane who never accepted the direction in which the denomination had taken them, but these were rare.

In the 1960s, when the civil rights movement in United States was in full swing, the black churches were at the forefront of the struggle. Martin Luther King's letter from Birmingham City Jail specifically argued on *theological* grounds against racial discrimination. King was a Baptist, but Pentecostal churches in the

United States, particularly black ones, followed his lead. In the generational changes after the victories of civil rights legislation, black Pentecostals worked hard to make up the educational deficits of the previous years while being conscious that many in their community struggled against endemic crime and poverty. In the academic world, emerging black scholars published on a range of topics and threw a light on black history. As a black Pentecostal middle class came into being in the 1990s, black televangelists like Fredrick Price, Creflo Dollar, and T. D. Jakes proclaimed messages of prosperity and, in the case of Jakes, emotional and spiritual healing, especially for women. *Woman, thou art loosed!* sold widely and became the theme of an annual conference. Black and Hispanic Pentecostal women also began to be heard in the academy and, through their work, the contribution of women within the early years of the Pentecostal movement was re-illuminated.

Historians and analysts of Pentecostalism recognized its multiple origins. Walter Hollenweger has argued that the 'black root' of Pentecostalism was responsible for its oral liturgy and its music. The characteristic openness of the Pentecostal meeting where anyone can stand up and testify to the power of God in their lives, may have affinities with the informal slave religion of the southern plantations within the United States. Equally, the musical motifs within Pentecostalism may be linked to jazz and blues because the interface between popular black culture and Pentecostalism is permeable. David Daniels put forward the view that Pentecostal denominations in the United States might be analysed through their music rather than through their doctrine. By this, he meant that the similarity between two denominations might be best established by listening to the typical sounds and rhythms of their worship rather than by looking at the wording of their doctrinal statements. A kind of historio-geographical chart of ecclesiastical relationships could be established in this way.

In another reflection that is partly linked to race, Harvey Cox has argued that Pentecostalism is potent because of its ability to tap into 'primal spirituality'. Such spirituality is expressed in speech through speaking or singing in tongues, in piety through the resurgence of dreams, visions, dance, healing, drama, and 'other archetypal religious expressions', and in hope through a belief in the Second Coming of Christ that inspires an expectation of a radically new and better future. For Cox, human beings are inescapably religious – we are *homo religiosus* – and the persistent suffering of African-Americans has induced a spirituality that 'leaped across the racial barrier and became fused with similar motifs in the spirituality of poor white people'.

Whatever its connections with the early history of Pentecostalism, race also offers a lens by which to view the great population migrations after 1945. Unprecedented movements across the globe have taken place in several directions. There has been a shift northwards from Africa into southern Europe and from Asia to the West, sometimes by multiple migrations of the same person and sometimes by migrations over two or more generations. American civil rights legislation in the 1960s had the unexpected effect of permitting settlement in the United States, an effect that was slowly taken up by distant Asian and Hispanic populations. In Britain, Commonwealth ties prepared the way for migration to the UK (about 425,000 Africans emigrated to Britain between 1971 and 2001) and, within Europe, the abolition of many border controls after the Schengen agreement ensured that access to one part of Europe allowed access to all parts. Only after the attacks of 9/11 were these trends re-examined. As a consequence of migration, there are at least 600 African congregations in Germany, a smaller but significant number in the Netherlands, and an unknown number in London and other parts of the UK. The largest congregation in London is Kingsway International Christian Centre, with deep roots in the African-British community. Many of the African migrants bring with them a vibrant Pentecostalism and an attitude to migration that allows them to see themselves not as poor refugees but as bringers of the faith that Europe once had and has now lost. In many instances,

Africans from Ghana and Nigeria were first evangelized by Europeans in the years after the 18th-century Methodist revival. These new congregations bring with them a range of spiritual beliefs but those which are Pentecostal, while they may incorporate rituals into their worship, hold essentially similar doctrines to those developed by European Pentecostals. In some cases, these migrant churches come from areas that have experienced Christian–Muslim conflict (as in Nigeria), with the result that they are sensitized to the political implications of European multiculturalism and keen to seize the opportunities representative democracy offers them. Their attitude, unlike that of the indigenous population, which in the main shows a bored indifference to politics, is more assertive and alert.

Political involvement

British and European Pentecostals may be about to begin to turn their attention to politics (the American Pat Robertson is discussed below). The spur to political action is usually found in a perception of injustice. In Latin America, carefully calibrated racism resulted in the upper echelons of society being made up of direct descendants of Spanish or Portuguese invaders and the lower echelons being made up of the descendants of the native population with an admixture of imported African slaves. The Spanish and Portuguese invaders were uniformly Roman Catholic and saw themselves on a divinely endorsed mission. By the mid-16th century, there were eight dioceses in Mexico and three in South America. Despite revolutionary upheavals in the great landmass stretching from Mexico down to the Southern Cone, the overall story is of the emergence of separate countries where folk Catholicism was firmly established by the 19th century. The United States, a Protestant power, slapped the old European colonial powers in the face by officially recognizing the newly independent South American countries and trading with them. The first Protestant missionaries appear to have been Methodists arriving from the United States in the 1880s and 1890s.

Pentecostals reached a variety of Latin American countries before the 1920s (see Chapter 3) but often faced fierce Catholic-inspired resistance.

After Vatican II, the situation eased and, in any case, Pentecostal mass evangelism had by then strengthened its churches and spread its message. After 1968, at an Episcopal conference at Medellin in Colombia, the Catholic Church began to formulate its policy of a 'preferential option for the poor' undergirded by a liberation theology that combined elements of Marxist analysis with great biblical themes like redemption from slavery. Even so, it was said that while the Catholic Church opted for the poor, the poor opted for the Pentecostals. By 2006, it was estimated that up to 30% of the total population of Chile were Pentecostals or charismatics, and that as many as 49% of the total population of Brazil had been affected by Pentecostal and charismatic renewal. The percentages could be higher in Guatemala. Though these figures may be over-inflated, the undoubted growth of Latin American Pentecostalism has been interpreted by those on the political left as being fuelled by US imperialism, a charge that is supported by pointing to financial links between Pentecostal organizations in Latin America and those in the United States. Against this interpretation must be set the meagre financial support given to early Pentecostal missionaries and the early indigenization of self-governing Pentecostal congregations. Often, Pentecostals were more interested in the next world than in this one: they were careless of politics and pinned their hopes for improving social conditions on gospel preaching and the moral transformation of individuals.

It is important to stress that not all Pentecostals think the same way about political issues and that there are distinctions to be drawn between neo-Pentecostals or charismatics who tend to be middle class and in favour of business and prosperity, and classical Pentecostals who tend to be poorer or rural or less educated and inclined to support the left. In Chile, the largest Pentecostal

Church in Santiago was opened by General Pinochet; other Pentecostals demonstrated against his regime and were exiled or killed. In Nicaragua, there were pro- and anti-Sandinista Pentecostals. Similarly, evidence for political quietism among Pentecostals must also be offset by Pentecostal expressions of liberation theology. Although Pentecostals, along with other evangelicals, have fairly straightforward political involvement in Colombia, Nicaragua, and Venezuela, in Brazil the most sophisticated Pentecostals maximize their influence by endorsing candidates across a range of political parties. In 2002, the caucus belonging to the Universal Church of the Kingdom of God contributed 22 members to Congress out of a total of the 60 or so evangelicals who were elected.

The political dynamics in Asia have been moulded by imperial China and imperial Japan as well as by trading routes leading west and multiple island territories like those of the Philippines and Indonesia. European power, either civil or religious, never dominated eastern Asia in the way that it dominated Latin America. Instead, Pentecostalism in Asia has built upon Protestant mission in the 19th century and, where this mission was Presbyterian or Methodist, converts were educated so they could become congregational leaders. As a result, both in the Philippines and Korea during periods of Japanese rule, the churches were one of the few reservoirs of patriotic sentiment that could survive foreign domination. In the Philippines, Pentecostalism quickly became indigenous and, after liberation from the Japanese after 1945 and the charismatic movement of the 1960s, many new congregations and Bible schools were founded. To give one example, the Jesus is Lord Church was founded in 1978 by Bishop Eddie Villanueva, previously a radical Communist activist. By 1999, it had grown to a multi-ministry network reaching across into Asia, Europe, Africa, the Middle East, and the United States. It claimed a total of two million members and owns a television station that broadcasts its services regularly. Villanueva endorsed one of the presidential candidates in the 1998 presidential election and hosts a weekly television show that addresses religious, social, and political issues. He has campaigned against pornography and is prepared to challenge government policy. Because his is a Filipino church, and not dependent upon foreign money or missionaries, its voice is seen as an authentic expression of popular concern.

In China, the effects of Pentecostalism are hard to calculate because the numbers of Pentecostals are uncertain. It is clear that, during the Maoist period of Communist repression, the authorities attempted to control Christianity by registering congregations and monitoring church activity. As a result, many Christians 'went underground' and met in homes or prisons where they adopted an ascetic, simple, and spiritual Christianity that relied upon the Holy Spirit. When China became more open and religiously liberal in 1979, rapprochement between the registered and persecuted Christians was hard to achieve. Consequently, Christianity in China flows in several streams and, though its Pentecostal form may reach as many as 50 million people, the most obvious result of its presence is to encourage transnationalism. This may be most easily seen in Hong Kong, since the Pentecostals who remained after Britain's hand-back to China see their duty as being to work for reconciliation with the mainland population while, at the same time, maintaining their connections with the worldwide Pentecostal movement.

Southern Korea was heavily impacted by a positive Pentecostal message that has led to Korean missionary work reaching out into Japan, Thailand, Africa, and elsewhere. The upbeat proclamation of the 'gospel of blessing' resonates in Asian culture and stands against a type of fatalism that is expressed by a reckless belief in the power of luck. Indeed, the gospel of blessing cuts against Buddhist astrological constraints and the weight of ancestral respect demanded by Confucian culture. Pentecostal Christianity

18. Jackie Pullinger: her ministry to drug addicts in Hong Kong is an example of progressive Pentecostalism

functions as a modernizing force that is challenging to the default cultural position in nearly all Asian countries. In India, Pentecostal evangelism has been especially successful among the Dalits, whose low-caste status (despite the illegality of the caste system) has historically rendered them suitable only for menial and dirty tasks. A message that denies the reality of *karma* and proclaims the universal and unmerited love of Christ confronts many of the presumptions of Hinduism and carries an implicit socio-political charge.

In all these continents, Pentecostalism builds churches and organizes them. It encourages literacy because it encourages Bible reading. It creates public and semi-public roles for women, and fosters their empowerment either by spiritual gifts or by education. In its complex arrangements for church growth, it will often, as a side effect, prepare its members for participation in democracy and entrepreneurialism.

Religious broadcasting

Religious broadcasting in the United States was developed upon a commercial model with a subsidiary public service function. Numerous radio stations sprang up and initially no single broadcaster commanded the airwaves, especially since the five time zones from the Atlantic to the Pacific fragmented scheduling. In Britain, a public broadcasting corporation (which in 1927 became the BBC), funded by a listeners' licence, reached the whole population simultaneously. In other parts of the world, other methods of funding were devised, although in many countries state control of broadcasting was the norm. As result, in the United States religious broadcasting was treated just like any other form of broadcasting in the sense that religious organizations could buy airtime if they wished. In Britain, religious broadcasting, in keeping with the religious temper of the day, was usually confined to the recording of a church service that emphasized the music of worship and ensured that preaching was unemotional. By contrast, in the United States, 'hot gospelling' was allowed.

Religious radio broadcasting was most vibrant in the United States, and in this Pentecostals played their part. By the late 1940s, when independent Pentecostal healing evangelists began to travel all over North America with their tents and crusades, television was beginning to open up. The healing evangelists had a dramatic event to communicate: not only was their preaching extempore and direct but, at the end of their meetings, they called people forward for prayer, and those who were ill received the evangelist's laying on of hands. If people on crutches or in wheelchairs received prayer and found themselves able to walk or run or in some other way immediately and visibly improved, the entire congregation was stirred and sceptical onlookers were surprised. The young Oral Roberts, with his portable 'canvas cathedral', prayed for thousands of people in this way, and a percentage appeared to have been dramatically healed and were prepared to testify to this in the revival atmosphere of his meetings as well as in local secular newspapers. When these events were captured on film, they could be broadcast on television. For many Americans, this was the 'old-time religion' that they had heard about from their pioneering grandparents.

Religious broadcasting of this kind combined musical showmanship and Bible teaching. It was a potent mixture, and Roberts, together with a group of Pentecostal evangelists coordinated through a ministry entitled Voice of Healing, never lacked for viewers. He soon built a multifaceted organization that poured out books, tapes, magazines, records, tracts, and broadsheets for mass distribution.

By the late 1960s, Roberts was prepared to abandon the preaching format and try a new approach. Away went the pulpit and in came the sofa. He went to an early version of the chat show that included music, lightweight interviews, soloists, celebrity appearances, and other trappings of what has become familiar on breakfast television or a thousand other magazine-style programmes. At first, Roberts was criticized by his core followers because some of the women on the show wore dresses with hemlines that were above the knee. Even so, his postbag was deluged with thousands of individual monthly contributions of finance. The new kind of religious broadcasting was quickly copied by other preachers and was acceptable to a better-educated stratum of viewers. This was the era of the charismatic movement when Pentecostal phenomena spontaneously appeared in mainstream middle-class churches in America. Roberts was completely in step with the times.

By the end of the 1990s, religious broadcasting, in a postmodern amalgam of styles, was being conveyed through downloads from websites, video-streaming, in podcasts and DVDs. Terrestrial, satellite, and cable television all carried the full range of religious content, some of it recycled from many years before, and the stranglehold of government or licence-paying control was broken. The internet filled with millions of items of religious data, making it possible to watch Pentecostal preachers or participate virtually in their services at any point of the day or night on every continent. American Pentecostals were seen in West Africa; West African preachers were seen in America; globalization made everywhere superficially the same. In this welter of possibilities, one of the major providers of Christian television in the United States, Trinity Broadcasting Network, began to broaden its appeal by commending its family-friendly materials. These were something that any family could sit down to watch without fear of embarrassment – violence, bad language, drug use, and sex scenes had been removed from any of the films or shows on offer. Additionally, editorial control of larger Christian providers ensured that whenever discussion on contentious topics like abortion or sexuality arose, a conservative position was respectfully advanced and only then balanced by a more liberal voice. On the secular channels, it worked the other way around. Pat Robertson, a charismatic who was a Republican presidential candidate in 1988, founded CBN (Christian Broadcasting Network) and added a further dimension: he would comment on the implications of world news or, if the Middle East were concerned, relate current events to his eschatological expectations.

Robertson's early surge in the presidential race appears to have been caused by his televisual celebrity. Yet, on individual policy issues, he fell well behind the other candidates and the voters soon dropped him. It may be that the number of viewers of Christian television was smaller than pundits realized and that this is why Robertson eventually faded. Or it may be that Christian viewers were simply unwilling to entrust their political destiny to the untried hands of a man without experience of government office. Later analysis of the linkage between religious broadcasting and politics concluded that Robertson's most lasting legacy may have been in bringing a fresh tranche of people into the democratic process, people who until that point had been uninterested in formal membership of political parties. Sarah Palin's showing in the 2008 presidential race may have stemmed from the support of these political virgins.

Conclusion

In countries like Russia in the period between the ascendancy of Lenin and the fall of the Berlin Wall, no political or social group was allowed to challenge the grip of the Communist party. But where there is sufficient freedom for opposition political parties, trade unions, and a civic sphere, Pentecostals may feel themselves mandated to move into politics, either as result of theological convictions about the extent of the kingdom of God or out of self-defence and to prevent persecution.

Religious broadcasting, at its simplest, is another form of gospel preaching, another way of communicating the message of Christ. In its more complex forms, it is a cultural phenomenon that combines religious belief with image-making electronic communication. It becomes a self-contained world with its own values and celebrities, its own marketable goods, and its own niche audience. It adds stature to international Pentecostal preachers and enables them to meet on equal status terms with minor politicians and major journalists. While its detractors may see it as right-wing imperialism, its defenders argue that it is a legitimate expression of free speech.

Only in racism has Pentecostalism betrayed its theological and spiritual values. Pentecostalism's very success has been dependent upon its belief that the Spirit of God has been poured out upon the whole human race. Any denial of this belief entails self-contradiction. For this reason, racism has been largely absent from Pentecostal history but, wherever countries have engaged in racist policies, Pentecostals have sometimes fallen to its toxic allure.

Chapter 8
Studies and surveys

Pentecostalism has been in existence for about 100 years and, from the beginning, been subject to academic study and empirical examination. Much of this investigation has been concerned with miracles, speaking in tongues, and prophetic utterances from a psychological point of view. In essence, the early studies of Pentecostal phenomena were largely hostile and associated them with pathological behaviour. More recent studies have been less judgemental and produced evidence for the therapeutic benefits of charismatic activities and the sanity or emotional stability of Pentecostals and charismatics. Since the year 2000, larger-scale statistical surveys addressed the phenomenon of Pentecostalism itself in an attempt to understand its progress and diversification and as a way of trying to predict its possible future trajectory.

Small-scale studies

Pentecostalism came into being more or less at the same time as Freudian psychoanalytic methods. The earliest academic studies understand speaking with tongues as evidence of an overflow from the unconscious mind and any claim to have heard directly from God as indicative of mental imbalance. These studies tended to be based upon very small numbers of people or even a single person and, despite the ingenuity of early psychiatric writers, the presuppositions of Freudianism were specifically anti-religious.

Later studies, particularly those after the 1960s when the charismatic movement had started, were better designed and might compare two matched groups, one of tongues-speakers and the other of non-tongues-speakers. These studies were able to show that tongues-speakers were just as balanced as non-tongues-speakers, and sometimes more so, and that speaking in tongues did not connect to trance-like states as had been previously thought. In any case, when the numbers of charismatics grew to many millions, it became increasingly difficult to assume that all of them displayed pathological symptoms. At the start of the 21st century, a series of studies by Leslie Francis investigated personality using the quantitative methods of practical theology and demonstrated the extrovert nature of many Pentecostal ministers, and could differentiate them from the generally more introverted ministers who were drawn to liturgical traditions.

Large-scale studies

The most sustained attempts to understand Pentecostalism on a large scale have come from David Barrett and his co-worker Todd Johnson. Barrett edited the first edition of the *World Christian Encyclopaedia* (published by Oxford University Press) in 1982 and summarized all the main statistics connected with world Christianity, both country by country and also by ecclesial megablocks: Roman Catholic, Protestant, Orthodox, non-white indigenous, Anglican, marginal Protestant, and Catholic (non-Roman). His monumental labours enabled him to place Christianity against the growth of the world population since the time of Christ and to make predictions from trends carried forward to the year 2000. He was able to show that in 1985 there were approximately 1.54 billion Christians, or 32.4% of the world's population, and that these numbers were poised to grow.

In the re-presentation of these figures related specifically to Pentecostalism and published in *The New International Dictionary of Pentecostal and Charismatic Movements*

(Zondervan, 2002), Barrett changed his categorization of groupings by viewing them as three historic waves of the Holy Spirit moving across the world. The first began in 1886 and produced the classical Pentecostal denominations which, by the year 2000, comprised 65 million people. The second wave, though it gained impetus in the 1960s, began in 1907 and comprised charismatics – those who spoke in tongues and believed in spiritual gifts but who remained in traditional denominations. These amounted to 175 million people. And, in the final wave, were a further 295 million who were made up of indigenous African Pentecostals, post-denominationalists, New Apostolics, and other apostolic networks. Altogether, he reached a grand total of 523 million, which he calculated amounted to 8.63% of the world's population. As he pointed out, such a vast array of people generated massive human and financial resources. He counted 740 Pentecostal denominations and 6,530 non-Pentecostal denominations with large internal charismatic sections, and all these were dispersed among 9,000 ethnic or linguistic cultures.

Even the United Nations does not possess a better set of figures than Barrett. What he sees is three spiritual waves, each with its

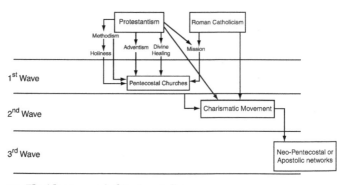

19. The 'three waves' of Pentecostalism

own separate characteristics. The classical Pentecostals are the most careful to define their doctrine and the most organized into denominational forms with mechanisms for establishing and propagating themselves. The charismatics live within traditional denominations, some of which are evangelical, and have in the past been the most educated but least strict about their exact Pentecostal beliefs. The third-wave churches are heterogeneous in organization and beliefs but frequently missional, authoritative, and radical. Each of the waves co-exists with the others, influences them, and grows at its own pace. The charismatics now outnumber the classical Pentecostals by about nine to one, and this has the effect of increasing the range of Pentecostal-style beliefs and practices – a diversity that may become wider when the profile of Christianity in China is fully revealed.

In 2006, the Pew Forum published a ten-country survey of Pentecostals and charismatics. Brazil, Chile, Guatemala, India, Kenya, Nigeria, the Philippines, South Africa, South Korea, and the United States were all surveyed by conducting face-to-face interviews, mainly using national samples of the populations. For instance, in Brazil, 700 members of the general public were interviewed along with 313 Pentecostals and 329 charismatics. This strategy allowed comparisons to be made between countries and between Pentecostals and charismatics, or either of these and the general population.

The picture that emerges from these figures confirms the prevalence of renewalists (the umbrella term for Pentecostals and charismatics). They make up about one-quarter of the world's Christians and, in countries with substantial Christian populations like Guatemala and Kenya, they amount to more than half the electorate. As many as 60% of renewalists in Asia attend church weekly, and this rises to 92% in Kenya, with the other countries in between. Religious television and radio are popular among renewalists (for instance, in Brazil 45% of Pentecostals and 20% of charismatics watch or listen daily), and over half say they have either experienced or witnessed divine healing of an illness or injury (the figure rises to 79% among Nigerian Pentecostals). In Latin America, as many as 45% (in Brazil) have converted from Roman Catholicism; in Nigeria, 2% converted from Islam, in South Korea 6% from Buddhism, and in India 7% from Hinduism. On social issues, renewalists are conservative. Homosexuality, prostitution, extramarital sex, polygamy, abortion, euthanasia, divorce, and suicide are all considered 'never justified' by a greater proportion of renewalists than is found in the general population. So, whereas 21% of the general population in Chile think that divorce is never justified, this figure rises to 31% among charismatics and 44% among Pentecostals. On the other hand, surprisingly, Pentecostals in Brazil are much more adamantly against drinking alcohol (72%) than they are against divorce (37%).

It is in financial and political matters that renewalist beliefs affect civic society. Renewalists tend to follow the economic complexion of their country: the majority of renewalists in the United States think they are better off in a free market, while in Chile it is only a minority which trusts this sort of capitalism. Yet, in every single one of the ten countries surveyed, more than half of renewalists believe that 'faith is very important to economic success', a belief that rises to over 95% among renewalists in the Philippines and Brazil. This faith is not to the exclusion of 'hard work', which also scores highly and is not motivated by mere acquisitiveness. However hard they work, renewalists in all ten countries are more likely than the general population to participate in 'social welfare services for the elderly, handicapped or deprived people'.

The centrality of renewalist beliefs to their lives is what marks them out from other Christians and most secularists. Faith applies to the whole of life and not merely to the few hours in the week or the month that may be allocated to public religious activity. Bertelsmann Stiftung's Religion Monitor is a questionnaire that has been completed by more than 21,000 respondents in

21 countries in a series of telephone or face-to-face interviews. In a series of items designed to tap into the centrality of religion for an individual's intellect, ideology, experience, and public and private practice, three of the counties with large renewalist contingents scored highly on the index. Though the study did not focus specifically on renewalists, the most recent report (2009) contains chapters on Nigeria and on Pentecostalism.

Nigeria is divided between a Muslim north and a Christian south. What the survey reveals is that the two religions are identical in some beliefs. In response to the item 'I believe that the end of the world is near', as many as 68% of Christians and 65% of Muslims 'totally agree'. In the same way, 69% of the Christians and 85% of Muslims believe in the 'efficacy of angels'. Similar patterns applied to belief in the 'efficacy of demons'. Pentecostals exorcize demons by prayer in the name of Jesus inspired by the Holy Spirit; Muslims by Quranic verses, holy water, and in the name of Allah. Although the figures given do not apply solely to Pentecostals, they are by far the largest group within the Nigerian sample, amounting to 45% of it. And, if it is true that Nigeria is 'Africa in miniature', these findings can be extrapolated to sub-Saharan parts of the continent. Consequently, the two religious blocks face each other with a similar expectation about the end of the world and of the spiritual forces that influence daily life.

Whether such findings can be extrapolated to Pentecostals in other parts of the world is more questionable according to other writers on the Religious Monitor. In the United States, while a small group of Pentecostals believes angels and demons are locked in a struggle for individual souls, this belief is not part of the background culture. As a result, Pentecostals in the United States who see life as a spiritual battle tend to be less concerned with exorcism and more concerned with politics, war, and economics, since these are the realms where spiritual forces are thought to be at work.

Implications of large-scale studies

Despite its uniform social conservatism, Pentecostalism has no fixed place on the political spectrum. In the United States, Pentecostals almost invariably vote Republican, whereas in Latin America Pentecostals, drawn predominantly from the poor, lean left. It would be a mistake to see Pentecostals as an extension of American 'soft power'; they are no more likely than their general populations to support the American-led 'war on terror'. Yet, there is one major global geopolitical conflict on which Pentecostals and charismatics converge with US policy: their reading of prophecy leads renewalists in all ten countries surveyed by Pew to be more supportive of Israel than their general populations.

When these findings are mapped onto demographic data relating to population growth, it is possible to offer credible future scenarios. In a series of books, Philip Jenkins has done precisely this. The first thing he notes in *The Next Christendom* (2002) is that the weight of world population by 2050 will have moved to the global south. Whereas in 1900, Europe, North America, and the former Soviet Union accounted for 32% of the world's population, by 2050 this figure will have shrunk to around 12%. Another way of putting this is by saying that in typical European countries about 16% of the population is aged over 65, whereas the comparable figure in southern nations is around 4%. By 2025, the countries with the largest Christian populations will be the United States, Brazil, Mexico, and the Philippines, followed by Nigeria, the Democratic Republic of Congo, Ethiopia, Russia, China, and Germany. The current style of Christianity within these countries will consequently determine the face of Christianity by the middle of the 21st century. Since renewalism is prevalent in many of these countries, that is how Christianity will look.

Aside from potential clashes with Islam over policy towards Israel, the majority of Christians in mid-21st-century Christianity are likely to share a positive attitude to material wealth and hard work while continuing to be supportive of social and community projects, especially if these projects are run from large congregations rather than by finance from the state. The experiential nature of renewalism generates doctrinal diversity and occasional extremes of behaviour as revivalist pulses ripple out from fluctuations in eschatological fervour. A perpetual drive towards mission will create megachurches in the new megacities of the world but, if the development of Pentecostalism over the 20th century is anything to go by, renewalists will welcome education. Asian seminaries are already producing biblical scholars competent in Greek and Hebrew and with a fine knowledge of church history. The new Christianity will be in touch with its roots. Future missionaries will be able to understand their own efforts in the light of historic patterns, and the first phase of mission is likely to be determined by linguistic factors. Already there are Brazilian Pentecostal missionaries working in Angola and Mozambique (because of a common Portuguese language), and the Chinese diaspora from other parts of Asia will reach further into China. Mexicans and Guatemalans will reach out into Spanish-speaking countries, while Americans will continue to access the English-speaking world, even if, as the most widely spoken language in the world at present, this language gradually has to compete with others.

Pentecostalism has become diverse and multifaceted while retaining a common experiential thread. The diversity is found more in church government than in doctrine, and the division between democratically governed congregations and apostolically governed networks is likely to continue. Running counter to these fault lines are unifying special events. The Pentecostal World Conference has met every two or three years since 1947 and its first task, drawing together delegates from major Pentecostal denominations, was to try to coordinate mission and relief work. The Pentecostal European Fellowship also operates at a denominational level but, beyond these, within the neo-Pentecostal networks there are international advisory bodies and many of these relate to national and international evangelical councils. Given that the beliefs of Pentecostals and neo-Pentecostals are similar, it is possible for them to worship together, enjoy the same books, listen to the same preachers, and be inspired by the same vision for the future.

Renewalism is likely to continue to generate the paradox of tight-knit sectarian groups and ecumenical initiatives. It may be that the World Council of Churches, which has so far lacked any major contribution from renewalists, will become a vehicle for a new form of inter-Christian cooperation. Equally, it is possible that some renewalists will jump the barriers and welcome inter-*religious* cooperation; beliefs about the universal influence of the Holy Spirit could open the way for major world religions to reach substantial areas of agreement. The prospects for inter-religious harmony and inter-religious conflict are balanced, and both may happen simultaneously.

In looking back on the 20th century, the Roman Catholic scholar Peter Hocken has noticed how messianic Judaism is almost invariably charismatic. He argues that this form of Judaism will be increasingly accepted within the church, with the result that the Jewish people who receive Jesus Christ will find a welcome within renewalist communities while continuing to protect their Jewish identities. This convergence between Judaism and charismatic Christianity holds the promise of liturgical innovation as well as a softening of theological edges within monolithic Roman Catholicism.

Conclusions

Pentecostalism and neo-Pentecostalism can expect to be subjected to continuing academic scrutiny. This is partly because they give rise to a variety of interesting and researchable topics about individual psychology, including healing, glossolalia, the effects of belief upon behaviour, intuitions of the future, emotion, and personality. It is also because Pentecostal congregations exist in many forms that are open to sociological inquiry, especially since these congregations interact with their own local cultures to create ever more new adaptations. Future studies of Pentecostalism are likely to be interdisciplinary and to attempt to integrate numerous perspectives into coherent wholes.

Beyond the academic study of Pentecostalism, its political and cultural effects are likely to excite contrasting interest both from those who support its generally conservative morality and its humanitarian enterprises and from those who oppose its religious foundations and its model of an interventionist God at work in a materialist world.

Further reading

History

Stanley M. Burgess and Eduard M. van der Maas (eds.), *The New International Dictionary of the Pentecostal and Charismatic Movements* (Grand Rapids, Mich.: Zondervan, 2002). This is a treasury of information, with articles on particular countries and theological topics and mini-biographical entries on individuals. There is also a very full statistical section.

Donald W. Dayton, *Theological Roots of Pentecostalism* (Peabody, Mass.: Hendrickson, 1987). A classic analysis of 19th-century Pentecostal roots.

William K. Kay and Anne E. Dyer (eds.), *A Reader in Pentecostal and Charismatic Studies* (London: SCM, 2004). This provides extracts from the writings of many Pentecostals and charismatics, arranged thematically.

William K. Kay, *Pentecostalism* (core text) (London: SCM, 2009). Provides a global overview of Pentecostalism against a discussion of history writing, the function of theology, and sociological theory.

Edith L. Blumhofer, *Aimee Semple McPherson: Everybody's Sister* (Grand Rapids, Mich.: Eerdmans, 2003). A sympathetic account of this controversial early Pentecostal preacher who made an impact on cultural life in the United States through broadcasting, appearing on Broadway, and by founding a denomination.

David Bundy, *Visions of Apostolic Mission: Scandinavian Pentecostal Mission to 1935* (Uppsala: Uppsala University Press, 2009). A big book full of information about the Scandinavian contribution to the early days of Pentecostal mission written by a multilingual scholar.

David E. Harrell, Jr, *Oral Roberts: An American Life* (Bloomington: Indiana University Press, 1985). A sympathetic but not uncritical biography of a key figure bridging the divide between holiness Pentecostalism and the charismatic movement.

Jack W. Hayford and S. David Moore, *The Charismatic Century* (New York: Warner Faith, 2006). An overview concentrating mainly on the United States.

Cecil M. Robeck, Jr, *The Azusa Street Mission and Revival* (Nashville, TN: Nelson, 2006). A well-researched but popular account of Azusa that covers the twists and turns in its history and includes a good portrait of W. J. Seymour.

Matthew A. Sutton, *Aimee Semple McPherson and the Resurrection of Christian America* (London: Harvard University Press, 2007). An account that goes beyond biography to show McPherson's political position as well as the legal wrangles that dogged her.

Vinson Synan (ed.), *The Century of the Holy Spirit* (Nashville, TN: Nelson, 2001). Mainly from an American perspective but useful as a starting point.

Grant Wacker, *Heaven Below* (Cambridge, Mass.: Harvard University Press, 2001). Well researched and giving an authentic flavour of early American Pentecostalism.

Allan Anderson, *An Introduction to Pentecostalism* (Cambridge: Cambridge University Press, 2004). A book that provides a global perspective with a great deal of detail.

Allan Anderson, *Spreading Fires: The Missionary Nature of Early Pentecostalism* (London: SCM, 2007). Uncovers the work of many half-forgotten missionaries who laid the foundation for Pentecostalism's global spread.

Allan Anderson and Edmond Tang (eds.), *Asian and Pentecostal: The Charismatic Face of Christianity in Asia* (Oxford: Regnum/Baguio City APTS Press, 2005). Contains valuable chapters written by indigenous Asian scholars.

Harvey Cox, *Fire from Heaven* (London: Cassell, 1996). Popular account with chapters focusing on aspects of Pentecostalism in various parts of the world.

Paul Freston (ed.), *Evangelical Christianity and Democracy in Latin America* (Oxford: Oxford University Press, 2008). An excellent overview.

Ondina E. González and Justo L. González, *Christianity in Latin America* (Cambridge: Cambridge University Press, 2008). Contains useful chapters on Pentecostals.

Ogbu Kalu, *African Pentecostalism: An Introduction* (Oxford: Oxford University Press, 2008). Written by an African, this text relates Pentecostalism to African ideas and presuppositions.

David Maxwell, *African Gifts of the Spirit: Pentecostalism and the Rise of a Zimbabwean Transnational Religious Movement* (Athens, OH: Ohio University Press, 2006). Thoroughly researched and by no means uncritical account of Pentecostalism in Zimbabwe within its wider African context.

David Martin, *Forbidden Revolutions: Pentecostalism in Latin America, Catholicism in Eastern Europe* (London: SPCK, 1996). A sociological account.

Amos Yong, *The Spirit Poured Out On All Flesh: Pentecostalism and the Possibility of Global Theology* (Grand Rapids, Mich.: Baker Academic, 2005). A wide-ranging and lucid text orientated towards systematic theology.

Theology

Kenneth J. Archer, *A Pentecostal Hermeneutic: Spirit, Scripture and Community* (Cleveland, TN: CPT Press, 2005). A book that shows how Pentecostal beliefs and interpretations are often cast in a narrative form and tested against the consensus of the congregational community.

Mark Cartledge, *Testimony in the Spirit: Rescripting Ordinary Pentecostal Theology* (Farnham: Ashgate, 2010). An in-depth study of the beliefs of people attending a long-established Pentecostal congregation in the UK. You hear the authentic voices of ordinary believers as well as the voices of a range of theologians.

Simon Coleman, *The Globalisation of Charismatic Christianity* (Cambridge: Cambridge University Press, 2000). Focus on Swedish neo-Pentecostalism written by a gifted anthropologist.

Paul Gifford, *African Christianity: Its Public Role* (London: Hurst, 2001). A thoughtful book based on extensive field work in West Africa.

Paul Gifford, *Ghana's New Christianity: Pentecostalism in a Globalising African Economy* (Indianapolis: Indiana University Press, 2004). Gives a clear idea of the profile and impact of the health and prosperity preachers of Ghana counterpointed against the perspectives of Mensa Otabil.

Veli-Matti Kärkkäinen (ed.), *The Spirit in the World* (Grand Rapids, Mich.: Eerdmans, 2009). Leading Pentecostal theologian brings together proposals to focus on the role of the Holy Spirit in diverse cultures.

Christopher J. Thomas, *The Devil, Disease and Deliverance* (Sheffield: Continuum, 1998). A thoughtful theological consideration of Pentecostal understandings of the causes of illness and the promises of healing.

Keith Warrington, *Pentecostal Theology: A Theology of Encounter* (London: T&T Clark, 2008). With an extensive bibliography and willingness to ground theology in the life of congregations rather than in history or philosophy.

Transformation video http://www.christian-witness.org/archives/van2001/video13.html accessed 16 August 2010. Provides vivid evidence of holistic approaches to social change and the claims of spiritual warfare.

Douglas Jacobsen (ed.), *A Reader in Pentecostal Theology* (Indianapolis, IN: Indiana University Press, 2006). Shows in verbatim extracts how diverse was early Pentecostal theology in the United States.

Frank Macchia, *Baptized in the Spirit: A Global Pentecostal Theology* (Grand Rapids, Mich.: Zondervan, 2006). An innovative account of the key Pentecostal tenet of Spirit-baptism that reworks the theme to expand its application.

Sociology

Estrelda Alexander and Amos Yong (eds.), *Philip's Daughters: Women in Pentecostal-Charismatic Leadership* (Eugene, OR: Pickwick, 2009). A set of theological and historical chapters on the leadership of women.

Donald E. Miller and Tetsunao Yamamori, *Global Pentecostalism: The New Face of Social Engagement* (Los Angeles, CA: University of California Press, 2007). An extensive series of interviews with Pentecostals all over the world reveals their involvement in humanitarian projects.

Walter J. Hollenweger, *Pentecostalism: Origins and Developments Worldwide* (Peabody, Mass.: Hendrickson, 1997). Hollenweger was the first major scholar of Pentecostalism to map its range and reach, and this book is a summation of his position.

Other studies

Leslie J. Francis, *Faith and Psychology* (London: Darton, Longman and Todd, 2005). Shows how an understanding of personality is relevant to studies of Christian ministry.

Peter Hocken, *The Challenges of the Pentecostal, Charismatic and Messianic Jewish Movements: The Tensions of the Spirit* (Aldershot: Ashgate, 2009). A charismatic Roman Catholic priest reflects on three 20th-century spiritual movements.

David Martin, *Pentecostalism: The World Their Parish* (Oxford: Blackwell, 2002). A complex series of sociological reflections on the reception of Pentecostalism in different parts of the world.

Philip Jenkins, *The Next Christendom* (Oxford: Oxford University Press, 2002). An account of Christianity that takes note of underlying population trends and credibly shows likely future scenarios.

Philip Jenkins, *The New Faces of Christianity: Believing the Bible in the Global South* (Oxford: Oxford University Press, 2006). Reading and interpreting the Bible varies enormously across the world.

Bertelsmann Stiftung (ed.), *What the World Believes: Analyses and Commentary of the Religion Monitor 2008* (Gütersloh, Germany: Verlag Bertelsmann Stiftung, 2009). Based on a survey of 21,000 people in 21 countries, a collection of scholars shows how religious belief and practice function in varying national contexts.

William K. Kay, *Apostolic Networks in Britain* (Carlisle: Paternoster, 2007). Shows how the new apostolic networks have arisen in Britain since 1970 and what their beliefs are.

Damian Thompson, *Waiting for Antichrist: Charisma and Apocalypse in a Pentecostal Church* (Oxford: Oxford University Press, 2005). An empirical and cultural study of a classical Pentecostal congregation, London City Church in Kensington.

Terry Virgo, *No Well-Worn Paths* (Eastbourne: Kingsway, 2001). An autobiographical account by a leader of one of the new apostolic networks.

Pew Forum http://pewforum.org/docs/?DocID=140 accessed 16 August 2010. An online review of a ten-country survey.

Academic journals on Pentecostalism

Pneuma (Brill), the journal of the Society for Pentecostal Studies.

Journal of Pentecostal Theology (Brill) discusses the theological dimension of Pentecostalism.

Journal of the European Pentecostal Theological Association discusses history and theology of Pentecostalism within and outside Europe.

Chronology

1860s onwards	Holiness becomes a predominant trend in Methodism
1887	The Christian and Missionary Alliance founded by A. B. Simpson promoting the 'Fourfold Gospel' of Jesus as Saviour, Baptizer, Healer, and Soon-Coming King
1901	Charles Parham at Topeka, Kansas
1902	Church of God is formed
1904/5	The Welsh revival (Evan Roberts)
1905	W. J. Seymour accepts Parham's doctrine
1905/6	Revival in Mukti, India (with P. Ramabai) and Pyongyang, Korea
1906/7	First General Assembly of the Church of God (Cleveland, Tennessee)
1906–9	Azusa Street revival, with W. J. Seymour as leader
1906	T. B. Barratt visits New York and then returns to Norway
1907	T. B. Barratt visits Sunderland Parish Church in the UK and people speak in tongues
1908	W. H. Durham visits Azusa Street
1909	Willis C. Hoover founds the Pentecostal Methodist Church of Chile
	Apostolic Church UK is formed in Wales
1910	W. H. Durham preaches 'finished work' doctrine in Chicago

1911	'Jesus only'/Oneness doctrine controversy (rejected in 1915 by Assemblies of God in the USA)
1914	Assemblies of God in the USA is constituted in Hot Springs, Arkansas
1915	W. F. P. Burton forms the Congo Evangelistic Mission
1923	Aimee Semple McPherson begins preaching in Los Angeles
1930	Kathryn Kuhlman gains recognition by opening Denver Revival Tabernacle
1939	First European Pentecostal Conference in Stockholm, Sweden
1947	First World Pentecostal Conference; David du Plessis from South Africa becomes general secretary for the World Pentecostal Conferences (until 1962); Donald Gee becomes editor of the Conference's paper *Pentecost* (until he died in 1963)
1948	Latter Rain Movement spreads from Canada
	Era of the healing evangelists in the USA
1950s	Early signs of the charismatic movement in Britain
1951	Full Gospel Business Men's Fellowship International is started in California
1953	Oral Roberts begins television ministry
1964	The Fountain Trust is established to encourage charismatic renewal among mainline churches, especially Anglicans; Michael Harper becomes its director
1965	Oral Roberts University is chartered
1967	Catholic charismatic renewal begins in Pittsburg, Pennsylvania
1975	*Charisma* magazine begins publication
1978	CBN University (now Regent University) is founded by Pat Robertson
1981	'Third wave' begins at Fuller Theological Seminary in California under John Wimber and taken up by C. P. Wagner (see diagram on page 122)

1993/	Toronto Blessing begins in Toronto Vineyard, Canada,
January	under John Arnott; visitors arrive from all over the world
1994	Cell Church movement gets underway in Singapore
1995	Roughly from this point Megachurches become more numerous

Index

A

Abrams, Minnie, 21, 51
Apostolic Faith Mission (AFM), 48, 87, 108
Africa, 1, 7, 10, 19, 31, 35, 45, 46, 47, 48, 50, 51, 67, 69, 72, 83, 87, 101, 105, 107, 108, 110, 113, 114, 118, 123, 125, 133, 138
AIC (African Initiated Church), 48
Anglicanism, 8, 9, 12, 21, 36, 37, 38, 39, 40, 47, 86, 121, 138
Angola, 47, 127
Asia, 1, 7, 21, 40, 43, 72, 83, 89, 102, 105, 110, 113, 123, 127, 132
Assemblies of God, 30, 31, 41, 46, 51, 55, 63, 82, 107, 138
Australia, 14, 35, 45, 69
Azusa Street Revival, 17, 23, 25, 26, 27, 28, 30, 31, 34, 36, 37, 41, 42, 48, 53, 85, 107, 108, 132, 137

B

Baptism in the Spirit, 28, 30, 31, 58, 59, 62, 64, 88
Barratt, T. B., 36, 37, 38, 137
Barrett, David, 2, 121
Bartleman, Frank, 25, 31, 107
Bellah, Robert, 104

Berg, Daniel, 41, 51
Bertelsmann Stiftung's Religion Monitor, 124
Bhengu, Nicholas, 48, 50
Boddy, Alexander A., 36, 38, 45, 68, 137
Bolivia, 10
Bourdieu, Pierre, 67
Brazil, 10, 51, 53, 83, 101, 112, 113, 123, 124, 126, 127
Broadcasting, 32, 45, 95, 100, 116–119
Bruce, Steve, 103
Buddhism, 44, 124
Bulgaria, 40
Burton, William F. P., 48

C

Calvinism, 11, 81
Canada, 10, 19, 35, 50, 85, 138, 139
Charismata, see Charismatic gifts
Charismatic gifts, see speaking in tongues, healing, prophecy
Chikane, Frank, 108
Chile, 10, 51, 112, 123, 124, 137
China, 1, 20, 31, 36, 40, 41, 42, 43, 75, 113, 114, 123, 126, 127
Cho, Yonggi David, 44, 65, 92
Church of God, 30, 41, 81, 107, 137

Church of God in Christ, 30
CMA (Christian and Missionary Alliance), 42
Cook, R. F., 41
Cox, Harvey, 109, 132
Cullis, Charles, 59

D

Dalits, 115
Daniels, David, 109
Darby, J. N., 12, 13
Denmark, 19, 36
Dispensationalism, 30, 61, 74, 75, 79
Dollar, Creflo, 109
Dowie, Alexander, 14, 38, 48
Du Plessis, David, 69, 87, 138
Durham, William, H., 28, 31, 37, 59, 137, 138

E

Ecclesiology, 79–87
Edwards, Jonathan, 11
Eschatology (end time), 6, 11–13, 25, 42, 73, 75–79, 118, 127
Ethiopia, 46, 126
Europe, see also individual countries, 10, 18, 20, 35, 36–40, 72, 103, 110, 113, 126
Exorcism, see also spiritual warfare, 69, 71, 72, 125

F

Finney, Charles, G., 15
Finland, 19, 36
Fletcher, John, 11
Ford, David, 106
Fourfold gospel (or foursquare gospel), 18, 60, 137
Fivefold gospel, 60
France, 19, 35, 39, 69
Francis, Leslie J., 121

Full Gospel Businessmen International, 67
Fundamentalism, 30, 34

G

Garr, A. G., 42
Gee, Donald, 83, 138
Germany, 19, 37, 38, 47, 77, 110, 126
Ghana, 50, 67, 111, 133, 134
Glossolalia, see speaking with tongues
Greece, 39
Guatemala, 101, 112, 123

H

Healing, 1, 13–14, 16, 23, 25, 27, 41, 43, 45, 46, 50, 55, 59–61, 67–69, 81, 82, 85, 86, 92, 109, 110, 116, 117, 124, 128, 138
Hocken, Peter, 128, 135
Holiness, see also sanctification, 14–15, 18, 23, 25, 27, 28, 30, 41, 43, 58, 59, 99, 105
Hollenweger, Walter J., 109, 134
Hong Kong, 31, 42, 43, 114
Hoover, Willis, 51

I

Iceland, 36
India, 10, 21, 31, 35, 40, 41, 43, 51, 69, 101, 115, 123, 124
Industrial Revolution, 10
Iglesia Metodista, 51
Irving, Edward, 12, 63
Isaiah, 60
Israel, 11, 13, 63, 75, 77, 92, 126
Italy, 35, 37, 38

J

Jakes, T. D., 109
Japan, 31, 35, 40, 113, 114

Jeffreys, George, 39, 82
Jenkins, Philip, 126, 135
Johnson, Andrew G., 36
Johnson, Todd M., 121
Julian of Norwich, 8

K

Kensington Temple, 78
Kenya, 47, 123
Keswick Movement, 21, 58
King, Martin Luther, 108
Korea, 21, 44, 90, 113, 114, 123, 124
Kraft, C. H., 71

L

Lake, John G., 48, 107
Lancaster, Sarah, 45
Last Days, see also eschatology, 5, 6, 35, 73
Latin America, 1, 72, 83, 89, 105, 111, 112, 113, 124, 126, 132, 133
Latter Rain, 85, 138
Lindsey, Hal, 77
Livesey, Lawrence, 41
Los Angeles, 17, 23, 24, 25, 27, 32, 55, 107, 134, 138
Luther, Martin, 8, 9,
Lutheranism, 8, 10, 36, 37, 86

M

Martin, David, 105, 133, 135
Mason, C. H., 30
McIntosh, T.J. and A., 42
McPherson, Aimee Semple, 32, 131, 132, 138
Megachurch, 46, 89–100, 104, 105, 127
Methodism, 1, 8–10, 14–16, 18, 21, 23, 25, 27, 28, 36, 38, 39, 43, 44, 47, 51, 55, 58, 68, 80, 81, 86, 111, 113, 137

Mexico, 10, 51, 53, 54, 55, 56, 111, 126
Miller, Don, 100, 102, 134
Mok Lai Chi, 42
Montanus, 7
Montgomery, Carrie Judd, 59
Moody, D. L., 13, 55
Moravians, 8, 9
Mozambique, 47, 127
Mukti revival, 21, 41, 51
Mumbai, 21
Müntzer, Thomas 8

N

Netherlands, The, 19, 38, 110
New York, 55, 95, 132, 137
New Zealand, 35, 46, 69
Nicaragua, 113
Nigeria, 50, 67, 111, 123, 124, 125, 126
Norway, 19, 36, 50, 137

O

Olazábal, Francisco, 54, 55
Oneness Pentecostalism, 31, 53, 63, 64, 138
Orthodoxy, 39, 40, 121
Otabil, Mensa, 67, 134
Otis, G., 71

P

Pakistan, 35, 40
Palin, Sarah, 119
Palmer, Phoebe, 14, 15
Parham, Charles Fox, 23, 26, 27, 58, 75, 137
Peretti, Frank, 72
Persecution, 43, 77, 119
Pethrus, Lewi, 37, 82
Pew Forum, 123, 135
Philippines, 40, 44, 113, 123, 124, 126

Index

Pietism, 1, 8, 36, 37
Polman, Gerrit R., 38
Progressive Pentecostalism, 99–103
Prakasam, J., 41
Price, Fredrick, 109
Prophecy (contemporary), 27, 83, 85, 87
Prophecy (canonical), 74, 77, 126
Prosperity, 48, 64–68, 78, 102, 112, 134
Pune (Poona), 21
Pyongyang, 23, 44

R

Race, 27, 107–111
Ramabai, Pandita, 21
Rapture, see also eschatology, 13, 77, 78, 80
Revival, see also Azusa Street revival, Welsh revival, Mukti revival, 11, 15, 18, 21, 36, 42, 45, 46, 55, 58, 79, 85
Roberts, Oral, 15, 65, 116, 117, 132, 138
Robertson, Pat, 111, 118, 138
Russia, 36, 77, 119, 126

S

Salter, James, 48
Salvation Army, 32, 38, 39, 68, 80
Sanctification, see also holiness, 11, 15, 16, 21, 23, 25, 28, 58, 59, 60
Sandford, Frank, 23
Scandinavia, 36, 39, 48, 53, 69, 82
Scofield Reference Bible, 13
Secularisation, 95, 103
Seymour, William J., 23, 25, 26, 27, 28, 30, 34, 132, 137
Shanghai, 42
Singapore, 43, 89
South Africa, 47, 48, 50

South America, see also individual countries, 37, 51–55, 111
Soviet Union, 126
Speaking in tongues, 5, 12, 25, 27, 31, 36, 37, 42, 43, 58, 64, 73, 86, 120, 128
Spirit-baptism, see Baptism in the Spirit
Spiritual warfare, 50, 71–73, 134
Sunderland Conventions, 36, 38, 68, 137
Sung, John, 43
Sweden, 19, 36, 37, 39, 138
Switzerland, 19, 38, 47, 59, 69

T

Thailand, 114
Thompson, Damian, 78
Tomlinson, A. J., 81
Trinity (Trinitarian), 8, 31, 53, 63, 118
Trudel, Dorothy, 59
True Jesus Church, 43
Turkey, 7

U

United States, 9, 10, 14, 17–21, 26, 30, 36, 42, 53, 55, 58, 59, 63, 69, 77, 99, 103, 108, 109, 111, 112, 116, 123, 124, 126
Uruguay, 10

V

Venezuela, 10, 113
Villanueva, Eddie, 113
Vingren, Gunnar, 51
Visions, 4, 5, 6, 21, 26, 110

W

Waves, three, 122, 123
Wagner, C. P., 71, 138

Welsh revival, 14, 16, 23, 36
Wesley, John, 8, 9, 10, 11, 14,
 15, 58
West Indies, 10, 35
Wigglesworth, Smith, 46,
 68, 87
Word of Faith, 64–68
World Council of Churches, 87,
 128
Wood, Alice, 55
Woodhead, Linda, 106
Woodworth-Etter, Maria B., 14

Y

Yamamori, Ted, 100, 102, 134
Yoido Full Gospel Church, 90, 92,
 95
Yunnan, 43

Z

Zimbabwe, 47, 51, 133
Zion, 14, 48
Zionism, 75

THEOLOGY
A Very Short Introduction

David F. Ford

This Very Short Introduction provides both believers and non-believers with a balanced survey of the central questions of contemporary theology. David Ford's interrogative approach draws the reader into considering the principles underlying religious belief, including the centrality of salvation to most major religions, the concept of God in ancient, modern, and post-modern contexts, the challenge posed to theology by prayer and worship, and the issue of sin and evil. He also probes the nature of experience, knowledge, and wisdom in theology, and discusses what is involved in interpreting theological texts today.

> 'David Ford tempts his readers into the huge resources of theology with an attractive mix of simple questions and profound reflection. With its vivid untechnical language it succeeds brilliantly in its task of introduction.'
> **Stephen Sykes, University of Durham**

> 'a fine book, imaginatively conceived and gracefully written. It carries the reader along with it, enlarging horizons while acknowledging problems and providing practical guidance along the way.'
> **Maurice Wiles, University of Oxford**

www.oup.co.uk/vsi/theology

ONLINE CATALOGUE
A Very Short Introduction

Our online catalogue is designed to make it easy to find your ideal Very Short Introduction. View the entire collection by subject area, watch author videos, read sample chapters, and download reading guides.

http://fds.oup.com/www.oup.co.uk/general/vsi/index.html

SOCIAL MEDIA
Very Short Introduction

Join our community
www.oup.com/vsi

- Join us online at the official Very Short Introductions **Facebook** page.
- Access the thoughts and musings of our authors with our online **blog**.
- Sign up for our monthly **e-newsletter** to receive information on all new titles publishing that month.
- Browse the full range of Very Short Introductions online.
- Read **extracts** from the Introductions for free.
- Visit our library of **Reading Guides**. These guides, written by our expert authors will help you to question again, why you think what you think.
- If you are a teacher or lecturer you can order inspection copies quickly and simply via our website.